Below: HMS *Mentor*, Hawthorn 'M' class, flying both the Red and White Ensigns.   *Swan Hunter*

Destroyers
of the
Royal Navy
1893-1981

Below: HMS *Bristol*, Type 82, showing complex superstructure.
MoD (Navy)

Destroyers
of the
Royal Navy
1893-1981

MAURICE COCKER

LONDON

IAN ALLAN LTD

D 23

First published 1981

ISBN 0 7110 1075 7

Published by Ian Allan Ltd, Shepperton, Surrey;
and printed by Ian Allan Printing Ltd at their works
at Coombelands in Runnymede, England

Below: HMS *Defender*, 'D' class, off Walney Island. *Vickers*

Contents

Below: HMS *Cardiff*, 'Towns' class, launching. Compare this photograph with HMS *Atherstone* for difference in shape of hull and superstructure. *Vickers*

Preface

The purpose of this book is to fill a gap in existing naval literature by being the first work to trace the history of the destroyer from its inception as a 'torpedo boat destroyer' to the guided missile versions of the modern RN. Each destroyer is described as it was accepted into service from the shipyard and, unless particularly noteworthy, later alterations and modernisations are omitted because of their number. Among the appendices are lists of the causes of loss of those destroyers sunk in the two world wars.

The destroyer has become a thing of the past now, for the current guided missile destroyers have little in common with the vessels of previous decades. Instead, the frigate, evolved during World War 2, is increasing in numbers, size and firepower. Therefore, I would dedicate this book to those vessels which may soon be just a memory — to the destroyers of the Royal Navy and all those who sailed on them.

Acknowledgements

I wish to mention with grateful thanks, the assistance and help which I have received from many sources amongst whom must be mentioned the following official organisations and individuals. Admiralty Departments (descriptions as in 1961), now Ministry of Defence (Navy): Department of the Chief of Naval Information; Material Branch I and Material Branch II; Admiralty Librarian and Staff; Ministry of Defence, Director of Public Relations (Navy) (Cdr F. E. R. Phillips, RN, Lt R. V. S. Neilson, RN); Office Services (Editing) (F. S. White, Esq); Naval Historical Branch (J. D. Brown Esq, Miss M. W. Thirkettle); The Fleet Air Arm Museum (The Curator, Lt-Cdr L. A. Cox, RN, and staff); Vickers Shipbuilding Group, Barrow in Furness (D. W. Robinson, Esq, Press and Public Relations Officer); Cammell Laird Shipbuilders Ltd (W. K. Fox, Esq, Assistant Manager-Information Services); The Royal Institution of Naval Architects (J. Rosewarn, Esq, Assistant Secretary (Administration), for permission to use material by the late Sir A. J. Sims from his paper 'Warships 1860-1960'); Real Photographs Ltd; Nashua Copycat Ltd; Sampson Low, Marston & Co Ltd, for permission to make use of various editions of *Jane's Fighting Ships;* E. F. Bunt, Esq; C. Turner, Esq; W. C. Turner, Esq; The Controller, Her Majesty's Stationery Office, for permission to use losses statistics from *Ships of the Royal Navy, statement of losses during the Second World War, 3rd September 1939-2nd September 1945,* HMSO 1947, also *Amendment No 1* to the above, HMSO 1949; Imperial War Museum, Department of Photographs (Mrs L. Willmot, E. Hine, J. Harding, and M. Willis, Esq); Swan Hunter Shipbuilders Ltd, Hebburn Shipyard (K. G. Burdis, Esq); J. Wilkinson, Esq, for photographs of the damaged HMS *Saumarez* and HMS *Volage*; Vickers Ltd, Millbank, London (M. J. Barry, Esq).

I am also grateful to Pauline for typing portions of this work and additionally being helpful and full of suggestions. If by neglect on my part I have omitted any person or organisation then I trust that my apologies will be accepted.

M. P. Cocker
New Moston, Manchester

Abbreviations

'A' Bracket	A metal bracket proud of the underwater hull holding the outer propeller shaft rigid	**mtg**	Mounting
AA	Anti-Aircraft	**M/V**	Motor Vessel
AS	Anti-Submarine	**nm**	Nautical mile
Calibre	The diameter of a projectile, eg 4.7in, 21in	**pdr**	Pounder
		P No	Pennant (Pendant) number
CP	Central pivot (a gun mounting)	**posn**	Position
DCT	Director Control Tower	**pp**	Length between perpendiculars
Displacement	The quantity of water in tons displaced by a ship	**QF**	Quick firing
		RAN	Royal Australian Navy
DP	Dual purpose	**RAS**	Replenishment at sea
E-Boat	A light tonnage (fast patrol boat) enemy surface craft	**RCN**	Royal Canadian Navy
		RDF	Radio Direction Finding
Full load	The displacement tonnage of a warship plus the weight of ammunition, fuel and stores	**RHN**	Royal Hellenic Navy
		RNN	Royal Netherlands Navy
		R/T	Radio Telephony
HA	High angle	**shp**	Shaft horse power
HIMS	His Imperial Majesty's Ship (Japan)	**SS**	Steam ship
HMAS	His Majesty's Australian Ship	**TB**	Torpedo Boat
HMCS	His Majesty's Canadian Ship	**TBD**	Torpedo Boat Destroyer
HMS	His/Her Majesty's Ship	**TC**	Torpedo Catcher
HP	Horse power	**TD**	Torpedo Destroyer
HSMS	High Speed Minesweeping	**TT(s)**	Torpedo tube(s)
ihp	Indicated horse power	**U-Boat**	Any enemy submarine
Is	Island/s	**wl**	Water line (length on)
LA	Low angle	**W/T**	Wireless Telegraphy
L(oa)	Length overall	**YD**	Yard (for shipbuilding yard)
MG	Machine gun		
mm	Millimetre		
MOD(N)	Ministry of Defence (Navy)		
MTB	Motor Torpedo Boat		

Below: HMS *Swift* at speed trials 1909. *R. Perkins*

Notes

Gunshields

In early classes, the gun was generally mounted upon a prepared deck base or platform and surrounded by canvas dodgers but these being obstructive a small plate shield of three sides and top was mounted over the gun breech and dropped to the line of the recoil barrel. Later shield designs were more elongated and extended to within a few inches of deck level. Later still the shield extended further back until all that was needed was a back plate and the turret was completed as in the 'Lightning' class.

Leaders and Classes

Between the wars, classes were built in eights with a specially designed leader to bring the class to nine (example 'H' class 1936). During 1939-45, the classes were built in eights and one of this number was selected to be leader (example 'S' class 1942).

Pennant Letters and Numbers

Originally numbers were given on naval stations and ships changed their numbers on passing from one station to another. About 1910 the Admiralty took the matter in hand and compiled a Naval Pennant List. Ships were grouped under the distinguishing flag of the type — TBs under the Red Burgee, destroyers under the Flag Superior H, and so on. Ships with nucleus crews in the 2nd or 3rd Fleets had a distinguishing letter to indicate the manning port, D — Devonport, N — Nore, P — Portsmouth. This ceased during World War I. At the start of World War II, there were more destroyers than could be accommodated under one flag superior, and they were numbered D00 to D99, F00 to F99 and H00 to H99.

The list in use today, D for destroyers, F for frigates, is published in *Jane's Fighting Ships* with which most readers will no doubt be familiar.

Nomenclature — Descriptive Title

The naming of HM Ships and the type of ship is no part of the subject of this book, but it will be noted that after the torpedo boats were constructed, the vessels to counter the torpedo boats were described as torpedo catchers, torpedo destroyers, and even torpedo gun boats, none of these titles being in the writer's mind truly descriptive; therefore, the term torpedo catcher in this book refers to all ships designed to counter the torpedo boat prior to the advent of the torpedo boat destroyer. It is difficult to ascertain exactly when the name 'Destroyer' came into common usage as the term TBD was retained even in the Navy List until 1919. As early as June 1906 it was shortened to Destroyer when referring to Destroyer Flotillas, as opposed to individual ships. No one Admiralty fleet order lays down that one term or the other should be used but again in 1917, an order refers to 'TBD's' and a further order in 1919 refers to 'Destroyers'.

Below: HMS *Codrington*, Admiralty leader. *R. Perkins*

Introduction

One of the many species of fish which abound in the oceans of the world is the 'Torpedo', otherwise known as the ray or electric ray, and the purpose of its inherent electricity is to disable, halt and immobilise the other fish which are its neighbours and prey. Perhaps therefore it is fitting that an underwater weapon now so well known and extremely effective should have been named thus more than a century ago.

In fact what we know as mines were also identified as torpedoes and the theory of underwater destruction of the enemy's vessels was appreciated as early as 1850. Very little progress, however, had been made towards making the torpedo into a self-propelled destruction charge, and it was not until the year 1866 that the English manager of an Italian engineering firm invented the true torpedo which is still the same in its essential principles as when Robert Whitehead first successfully completed his trials of the 'Hydrostatic Torpedo'.

Four years later, the Admiralty commended the weapon to Parliament and the manufacturing rights were purchased for the sum of £15,000. In 1877, HMS *Shah* unsuccessfully attempted to torpedo a Peruvian naval vessel with which she was engaged in conflict.

The problem the Admiralty had now to face was how best to employ the new weapon. It was, as most agreed, a weapon of surprise and stealth and indeed at that time, with a speed of six knots, the odds were in favour of the attacked vessel escaping the somewhat erratic course of the torpedo which had a limited range of about four and a half cables. Therefore, attacks during the dark hours or in poor visibility were more favoured and carried out by the ship's launch with a torpedo slung on either beam and released at the appropriate moment.

It then became evident that, as the torpedo improved, the ships of the fleet of the time were not of sufficient speed to approach within torpedo range and retire without seriously exposing themselves to the enemy's gunfire. Therefore a small but comparatively speedy craft was designed and produced in some numbers, for just a foray, although the ships of the fleet retained their torpedo tubes (this being the approved mode of launching from large vessels), just in case they, too, might be sufficiently close to bring their new weapons to bear. The first torpedo boat, although built by Thornycroft, was ordered by the Norwegian Government in 1873 with a length of 57ft, displacement of 7.5ton and a speed of 15kts (on trials), but in 1877 HMS *Lightning* became the first Royal Naval torpedo boat with 19kts on the measured mile. Thereafter this type of vessel grew in size and numbers with the speed increasing steadily with power, and a typical torpedo boat of 1886 by White made 20kts on 1,100shp, displaced 125ton and carried three 14in tubes. So the evolution continued, for now it was evident that a host of such craft would well be a menace to any fleet.

As a remedy, a second type of small craft known as the 'torpedo catcher' was designed. The first for the Royal Navy was HMS *Rattlesnake* from Lairds in 1886, but they failed to live up to expectations possibly because they displaced 400-800 tons and were of insufficient speed to bring the torpedo boats to bay (see Appendix 3).

Below: HMS *Lightning* on builder's trials on the Thames 1877. *Vosper Thornycroft*

Above: The earliest torpedo boats, 1878. *IWM*

The next design type was named the 'torpedo boat destroyer' and, although a change of policy for the Admiralty, in destroying (or trying to) their own creation, it was initially successful, and when the need for seaworthiness rather than excessive speed was realised, then the destroyer design (as it was known) forged ahead and ousted the very craft it was to destroy. HMS *Havock* was the first destroyer to be commissioned and came from the Yarrow yards in 1893. It had two shafts driven by triple expansion engines and made 27kts. About 60 of these torpedo boat destroyers (or TBDs as they were known) were built to Admiralty specifications between 1893 and 1900, with slight improvements and modifications by the builders who had had a very free hand in the design. These formed the 'A' and 'B' classes.

By now the turbine had made its effect on the Admiralty by the appearance of the *Turbinia* at the 1897 Spithead Review, and in 1899 HMS *Viper* a vessel of 312 tons, made 37.1kts at 12,000ihp on trials. HMS *Viper* had

a formidable armament for a ship of 210ft: one 12-pounder, five 6-pounder guns and two 18in torpedo tubes. A similar boat to the *Viper* was HMS *Cobra* which had been completed by Armstrong-Whitworth (Tyne) but only had a short service career as she broke in two in 1901. Just over a month later HMS *Viper* was also lost, being wrecked on Alderney. After the *Cobra* and *Viper* losses, snake names were not repeated, although HMS *Rattlesnake* saw much service and was sold in 1921.

The trouble appeared to be that the long narrow-beamed hulls were under great stress with the tremendous power of the turbines and hard driving into short seas. When the destroyers grew beamier, then their seaworthiness improved.

Above: Torpedo catcher HMS *Rattlesnake* fitting out, 1877. *IWM*

The 'C' class was of no particular advance upon the earlier classes, and the boats were apparently constructed proportionately between four or five yards to Admiralty specifications, but the builders own designs. HMS *Velox* of this class had triple-expansion engines for cruising although relying on turbines for her main propulsive power.

The 'D' class followed — smaller and handier vessels and all to one design. Their appearance was improved for they each had two funnels and turtle back bows, the only differences being that four of them had outboard rudders. To continue in chronological order of entering service, HMS *Taku* was accepted into service from another source, and this is the proper place to mention that the Royal Navy received excellent service from ex-Chilean, Turkish, Portuguese and Greek destroyers during World War 1; and ex-Brazilian, French and Turkish vessels during World War 2 nor must we forget the 'Destroyers for Bases' which were as valuable in 1940. The majority of the 'ex' destroyers were new buildings, but a number were purchased outright or leased.

In 1907, HMS *Swift* was commissioned; she was a vessel far ahead of her time, not approached for size and power in destroyer-building until 1937, some 30 years later.

A note must now be made regarding the formation of the destroyer class system. The 'A', 'B', 'C', 'D', 'E', 'F', 'G', 'H' and 'I' classes did not exist as such until 1913 when the Admiralty enquired into the then existing method and system of destroyer names and naming and decided to introduce some uniformity by grouping all the existing 27kt ships of the 1890s into the 'A' class, and the 30kt boats which followed would form the 'B' class, and so forth to the 'K' class. The class to follow after 'K' would be 'L', and would have names commencing with that letter and all following classes would conform to the new ruling. The system worked well even though such a large class as the Admiralty 'M' had, due to its size, four initial letters allotted to it. Further large classes were the Admiralty 'R', 'S', 'V' and 'W', the 'R' class having three letters and the 'S' two. No 'J' class was formed until the

'Javelins' during the late 1930s. Two systematically named groups of boats were however the 'E-River' and the 'F-Tribal' classes of 1903-06.

The 'F' class were reasonably beamy ships with good speed, and the 'G' class were slightly larger but slower, notable for being the first destroyers to mount the 4in gun.

With the 'H' and 'I' classes, there was little overall change, although both mounted the 4in gun, there being two in the 'H' and 'I' boats and three in the 'K' class which had increased tonnage and speed on two or three shafts according to the builders' variations.

At the 'L' class, standardisation in build was virtually complete although the boats had either two or three funnels.

Increased tonnage again with armament and tubes were features of the Admiralty 'M' class (which also attained a record number of names to the class, there being a total of 85), and high speed was maintained although on three shafts.

Not unnaturally, the 'big three' destroyer constructors (Yarrow, Thornycroft and Hawthorn) supplied a small number of their own modified design vessels of most Admiralty classes, and they had also a little advantage in speed.

Two classes then followed composed completely of leaders, being ships which were of 1,500 tons and exceeding 320ft in length. These were the 'Marksman' and 'Anzac' classes of 1915-16.

In 1916, a virtual repeat of the Admiralty 'M' class was decided upon and in that year the first of the Admiralty 'R' class was completed. Ships of this class had more speed although only on two shafts, but all had geared turbines. The following large class in 1918 was called the Admiralty 'S' class, and maintained the previous standard of the 'R' class together with a larger bridge. HMS *Shikari* (which much later on had the distinction of being the first destroyer in the Royal Navy to have radar, albeit for evaluation) of this class was not completed until 1924, nor HMS *Thracian* till 1922.

Then followed what is probably the most famous class of all, the Admiralty 'V' class which became identified with the follow-up class, the Admiralty 'W' to form the 'V' and 'W' classes of both world wars. They were fine ships, to realistic designs and with perhaps the most significant step forward in gunnery mounting in that the guns were superimposed in the now familiar positions of A, B, X and Y.

With peace in late 1918, two further leader classes were under construction, these being the Thornycroft type and the Admiralty large design, and, apart from the 14 ships of the Admiralty modified 'W' class, were the first destroyers to mount the 4.7in gun.

Destroyer building slowed up tremendously and 38 ships of the last mentioned class were cancelled. In 1924 however, the Admiralty asked Yarrow and Thornycroft to design and construct one destroyer each to embody all the lessons of the past 31 years and World War 1. The two ships were known as the Experimental 'A' class, and these two destroyers were the prototypes of the long line of classes to be built in alphabetical sequence from the 'A' of 1929 to the 'Zambesi' class of 1944. They had greater endurance, and gunnery control, which really commenced with the 'V' and 'W', reached its greatest height in 1944 with the 'Later Battle' class which carried an American pattern of director tower. Further equipment fitted at intervals was really effective W/T and R/T with Asdic radar and other electronic devices of war.

Then followed the new 'A' class of 1929, and a destroyer of this class displaced about 1,400 tons and made 35kts plus at 34,000shp. The armament in the main consisted of 4.7in guns with lighter weapons such as 2-pounders and machine guns. The 'A' to 'Intrepid' classes were, with modification, of like build and design.

Mention must however be made of a one design class in 1929, this ship being HMS *Codrington* which, for her period, was all that was best in destroyer design. It should be noted also that since the Admiralty 'S' class of 1918, all destroyers were twin funnelled and had two pole masts with yardarms.

In 1937, however, a new concept in destroyer design was evolved which completely altered the outward appearance of this type of ship. These ships were named after tribes and suffered 50% losses during World War 2. The 'Tribal' class, as it was known, had a main armament of eight 4.7in guns in twin shields, mounted in the now familiar A, B, X and Y positions. This splendid design was followed by the 'Javelin' class which comprised three groups of eight ships, each of which had names commencing with either a J, K or N; the full class comprised 24 ships with eight to each of the letters.

Following was the 'Lightning' class with two groups of eight ships which had names commencing with either an L or M, and all were one-funnelled (as were the two previous classes) and with tripod masts. The 'M' group were destroyers 'par excellence' for not only were they most handsome looking but they were also the first ever to mount turrets for their main armament.

With the opening of hostilities with the Axis powers in 1939 the shortage of destroyers was acute until UK yards could deliver the large number of vessels under construction. Therefore the 'Destroyers for Bases' agreement was ratified with the United States and 50 'Flush Deckers' of 1918 vintage were delivered from American bases, although seven were immediately transferred to the Royal Canadian Navy.

In 1940 the destroyers were called upon to carry out a task for which they had certainly not been designed, yet 91,620 men of the British Expeditionary Force were evacuated home in the teeth of enemy opposition at Dunkirk.

From 1939, a short radius utility class had been under construction; known as the 'Hunt' class/es, they served well until and after the delivery of the first of the 'Obdurate' and 'Paladin' fleet destroyer classes. The 'O' class was well powered and fast, but as it had seemingly overtaken the Ordnance factories, the class had to mount the old type 4in gun.

The next two classes, 'Queensborough' and 'Rotherham', were of like design to the 'O' and 'P' classes, and all comprised eight ships each.

Following were the six utility construction classes commencing with HMS *Savage* (which bore in A position the prototype turret for the 'Battle' class) and ending with HMS *Zambesi*. The destroyers of these classes were all (with certain exceptions) armed with 4.7in guns in single shields. An innovation on the majority of these ships was the lattice or trellis foremast, and, about 1941, the first 'Hedgehog' anti-submarine weapon was mounted in HMS *Westcott*. With the 'Wager' or 'W' class of 1942, the 4.7in gun was mounted for the last time as the main armament of a destroyer, the 4.5in calibre of lower velocity being the replacement weapon, still at sea today.

Then came a large class of 32 destroyers which were allotted into four groups for naming purposes, these being the 'Ca', 'Co', 'Ch' and 'Cr' groups, the ships of which were not as the previous six classes and the last three groups had power worked main armament.

Meanwhile a new and powerful destroyer design was under construction named the 'Battle' class. They were ships with all main armament forward of the bridge, in two power worked turrets, being designed for tropical service and mounting a single 4in in a shield aft of the funnel. From the bridge aft was mounted a selection of heavy to light automatic AA weapons, not to forget the torpedo tubes — eight 21in as in most destroyers. They were large ships of 2,315 tons and length overall of 379ft. A later 'Battle' class was built, chiefly to the same designs but with improvements.

With the end of the war, destroyer building once again slowed and the 'Weapon' class of four ships was completed in 1948, this being a class which was like nothing that had gone before, reverting to two funnels and lower tonnage. Then followed a combination of 'Battle' and 'Weapon' designs to produce the 'Daring' class with square turrets for twin 4.5in guns and all welded construction, to produce the heaviest destroyer then known at 2,610 tons.

Finally there were the 'County' class guided missile destroyers which are definitely of light cruiser tonnage and similar to the Type 81s and have unique propulsion methods; the one and only Type 82 HMS *Bristol* with her three funnels; and the modern 'Town' class Type 42s with their improved follow-up class, the 'Stretched 42s', which are larger in all respects.

Details of all classes as completed, or as accepted will be found on the appropriate page.

Royal Naval Destroyers 1893-1981

Miranda

After the Admiralty had persuaded the UK Government to purchase the manufacturing rights for Robert Whitehead's torpedo, a vessel capable of carrying and using the weapon had to be found. Therefore Messrs J. I. Thornycroft were asked to fit the weapon afloat, which they did by building a river launch of light construction capable of 16kts with a side/stern launching device to aim the torpedo. *Miranda* was not commissioned but acted as a trials vessel for the torpedo and the knowledge gained led to HMS *Lightning* Torpedo Boat No 1.

'A' Class

Unit	Completed	Builder	Unit	Completed	Builder
Ariel	1896	Thornycroft	*Lynx*	1894	Cammell-Laird
Banshee	1894	Cammell-Laird	*Opossum*	1895	Hawthorn
Boxer	1894	Thornycroft	*Porcupine*	1895	Palmers
Bruiser	1894	Thornycroft	*Ranger*	1895	Hawthorn
Charger	1894	Yarrow	*Rocket*	1894	Clydebank
Conflict	1894	White	*Salmon*	1895	Earle
Contest	1894	Cammell-Laird	*Shark*	1894	Clydebank
Daring	1893	Thornycroft	*Skate*	1895	Vickers Armstrong (Barrow)
Dasher	1895	Yarrow	*Snapper*	1895	Earle
Decoy	1894	Thornycroft	*Spitfire*	1895	Vickers Armstrong (Tyne)
Dragon	1894	Cammell-Laird	*Starfish*	1894	Vickers Armstrong (Barrow)
Ferret	1893	Cammell-Laird	*Sturgeon*	1894	Vickers Armstrong (Barrow)
Fervent	1895	Hanna Donald & Wilson	*Sunfish*	1895	Hawthorn
Handy	1894	Fairfield	*Surly*	1894	Clydebank
Hardy	1894	Doxford	*Swordfish*	1895	Vickers Armstrong (Tyne)
Hart	1894	Fairfield	*Teazer*	1895	White
Hasty	1894	Yarrow	*Wizard*	1895	White
Haughty	1895	Doxford	*Zebra*	1895	Thames Iron Works
Havock	1893	Yarrow	*Zephyr*	1895	Hanna Donald & Wilson
Hornet	1893	Yarrow			
Hunter	1895	Fairfield			
Janus	1895	Palmers			
Lightning	1895	Palmers			

Below: HMS *Dasher*, 'A' class torpedo boat destroyer, at sea in 1901. *R. Perkins*

Displacement: 260 tons
Length: 200ft
Breadth: 19ft
Draught: 7ft
Armament: *Main* One 12pdr
Secondary Five 6pdr
Tubes Two/three 14in
Machinery: Triple expansion on two shafts giving 4,000shp
Max speed: 27kts
Fuel: 60 tons coal

Class Notes

Ships of this class were not all alike in appearance, the number of funnels varied from ship to ship. The bows towards the waterline tended to swell out into the familiar 'ram' shape of the period. Another recognition point was the turtle-back topped forecastle which was intended to clear the bow but actually dug them in in anything of a sea.

Above: Painting of HMS *Havock*, 'A' class, at sea. *Yarrow*

Some of the class, including HMS *Havock*, had locomotive boilers built into them. The correct marine boilers replaced these at a later date.

HMS *Daring, Decoy, Ferret, Havock, Hornet* and *Lynx* were built with a bow torpedo tube which tended to make them very wet.

Historical Notes

HMS *Boxer* collided with HMS *Decoy* on 6 February 1918.
HMS *Havock* was later converted into the first submarine depot ship.
HMS *Lightning* struck a mine on 30 June 1915 in the North Sea.

'B' Class

Unit	Completed	Builder
Albacore	1908	Palmers
Arab	1901	Clydebank
Bonetta	1908	Palmers
Earnest	1896	Cammell-Laird
Express	1896	Cammell-Laird
Griffon	1896	Cammell-Laird
Kangaroo	1901	Palmers
Lively	1901	Cammell-Laird
Locust	1896	Cammell-Laird
Myrmidon	1901	Palmers
Orwell	1901	Cammell-Laird
Panther	1897	Cammell-Laird
Peterel	1899	Palmers
Quail	1895	Cammell-Laird
Seal	1897	Cammell-Laird
Sparrowhawk	1896	Cammell-Laird
Spiteful	1898	Palmers
Sprightly	1901	Cammell-Laird
Success	1901	Doxford
Syren	1901	Palmers

Unit	Completed	Builder
Thrasher	1896	Cammell-Laird
Virago	1896	Cammell-Laird
Wolf	1897	Cammell-Laird

Displacement: 355-470 tons
Length: 210ft
Breadth: 21ft
Draught: 5ft 6in
Armament: *Main* One 12pdr
Secondary Five 6pdr
Tubes Two 18in
Machinery: Triple expansion on three shafts giving 6,000shp
Max speed: 30kts
Fuel: 80 tons coal

Class Notes

The 'B' class torpedo boat destroyers, being of one third greater tonnage than the 'A' class although of similar armament, had the advantage of three knots from 'down

Right: HMS *Locust*, 'B' class, leaving harbour, 1908. *R. Perkins*

Below right: HMS *Thrasher*, 'B' class, at anchor, 1897. *R. Perkins*

below' in excess of the previous class. They also had more of a unified appearance, each having four funnels, although their spacing was different. Although rated for 30kts, speed had to be reduced in even mediocre weather and the class had little reserve hull strength. *Albacore, Arab, Bonetta* and *Express* were turbine-powered giving 6,000-9,000shp making 26.75-31kts.

Historical Notes

HMS *Myrmidon* was lost by collision with the SS *Hambourne* in the English Channel on 26 March 1917.

HMS *Success* was wrecked off Fifeness on 27 December 1914 and was the first destroyer lost in World War I.

'C' Class

Unit	Completed	Builder	Unit	Completed	Builder
Albatross	1898	Thornycroft	*Fairy*	1897	Fairfield
Avon	1896	Vickers Armstrong (Barrow)	*Falcon*	1901	Fairfield
Bat	1896	Palmers	*Fawn*	1897	Palmers
Bittern	1897	Vickers Armstrong (Barrow)	*Flirt*	1897	Palmers
Brazen	1896	Clydebank	*Flying Fish*	1897	Palmers
Bullfinch	1901	Earle	*Gipsy*	1897	Fairfield
Chamois	1896	Palmers	*Greyhound*	1900	Hawthorn
Cheerful	1897	Hawthorn	*Kestrel*	1898	Clydebank
Cobra	1900	Vickers Armstrong (Tyne)	*Lee*	1899	Doxford
Crane	1896	Palmers	*Leopard*	1897	Vickers Armstrong (Barrow)
Dove	1898	Earle	*Leven*	1901	Fairfield
Electra	1901	Clydebank	*Mermaid*	1898	Hawthorn

Unit	Completed	Builder
Osprey	1897	Fairfield
Ostrich	1901	Fairfield
Otter	1896	Vickers Armstrong (Barrow)
Racehorse	1900	Hawthorn
Recruit	1901	Clydebank
Roebuck	1901	Hawthorn
Star	1896	Palmers
Sylvia	1897	Doxford
Thorn	1901	Yarrow
Tiger	1901	Clydebank
Velox	1902	Hawthorn
Vigilant	1901	Clydebank
Violet	1897	Doxford
Viper	1899	Hawthorn
Vixen	1901	Vickers Armstrong (Barrow)
Vulture	1898	Clydebank
Whiting	1896	Palmers

Displacement: 355 tons
Length: 210ft
Breadth: 21ft
Draught: 9ft
Armament: *Main* One 12pdr

Top: HMS *Flying Fish*, 'C' class, making way entering harbour, 1909. *R. Perkins*

Above: HMS *Velox*, 'C' class, making way, 1904. *R. Perkins*

Secondary Five 6pdr
Tubes Two 18in
Machinery: Triple expansion on two shafts giving 6,000shp
Max speed: 30kts
Fuel: 80 tons coal

Class Notes
As with the 'B' class these ships were quite heavily armed, the 12-pounder being in A position forward of the bridge. The 6-pounders were positioned two each side aft of the first and third funnels and one on the stern. All ships had a light pole foremast with a short derrick immediately behind the conning position. The funnels were equidistant with the first and third of less diameter than the second but all being of the same height. The tubes were aft, one either beam.

HMS *Viper* and *Velox* were powered by turbines on four shafts with two screws, one inboard and one outboard of the A bracket on each shaft.

HMS *Cobra* featured an outboard rudder secured to the transom stern with the above-water section tapering to take a fitting for emergency steering.

Historical Notes

HMS *Bittern* was lost through damage sustained after collision with the SS *Kenilworth* off Portland Bill on 4 April 1918.

HMS *Chamois* was the victim of a rather unusual mechanical failure, in that the tip of a propeller blade broke off whilst the ship was underway and, due to its impetus, the fragment penetrated the underwater hull aft of the A bracket which caused filling and flooding of the stern and successive compartments until she foundered.

HMS *Cheerful* struck a mine on 30 June 1917 off the Shetlands.

HMS *Fairy* sank through damage sustained after ramming *UC-75* on 31 May 1918 in the North Sea.

HMS *Falcon* sank after collision with the *St John Fitzgerald* on 1 April 1918 in the North Sea.

HMS *Flirt* was lost in action with German destroyers on 27 October 1918, being torpedoed.

HMS *Recruit* was torpedoed by a U-boat on 1 May 1915 off the Galloper in the Thames.

HMS *Velox* struck a mine on 25 October 1915 off the Nab Light Vessel.

'Taku' Class

Unit: Taku (ex-*Hai Nju*)
Completed: 1898
Builder: Schichau (Elbing)
Displacement: 305 tons
Length: 194ft
Breadth: 20ft
Draught: 6ft
Armament: *Main* Six 3pdr
Tubes Three 18in
Machinery: Triple expansion on two shafts giving 6,500shp
Max speed: 30kts

Class Notes

The only vessel of this class to serve with the Royal Navy, HMS *Taku* was of low freeboard with two large, raked funnels and light pole fore and main masts. The bow was 'ram'-shaped and the hull had curved topsides for the greater part of the main deck.

Historical Notes

This vessel was taken over as a prize in 1900 from the Chinese Navy at about the time of the Boxer Rising. Named *Taku* to commemorate the attack on the forts of the same name in the same year, she was sold out of the Service at Hong Kong on 25 October 1916.

Below: HMS *Taku*, at anchor in Hong Kong, 1904. *R. Perkins*

'D' Class

Unit	Completed	Builder	Unit	Completed	Builder
Angler	1896		*Cynthia*	1898	
Ariel	1897		*Desperate*	1895	
Coquette	1897		*Fame*	1896	
Cygnet	1898		*Foam*	1896	

Unit	Completed	Builder
Mallard	1896	
Stag	1899	

Builders: Thornycroft
Displacement: 355-370 tons
Length: 210ft
Breadth: 21ft
Draught: 7ft 2.4in
Armament: *Main* One 12pdr
Secondary Five 6pdr
Tubes Two 18in aft
Machinery: Triple expansion on two shafts giving 5,800shp
Max speed: 30kts
Fuel: 80 tons coal

Class Notes

The ships of this class were the only ones of the 1896 building with two funnels, but in common with the 'B' and 'C' classes had as a recognition feature turtle-back topped bows and large ventilators between the funnels. Ships of this class saved considerable weight by being constructed from a new specification of steel which added strength to the hull.

Historical Notes

HMS *Coquette* struck a mine and sank on 7 March 1915 in the North Sea.

Below: HMS *Angler*, 'D' class, at sea in 1898.   *R. Perkins*

Bottom: HMS *Cygnet*, 'D' class, entering harbour 1909.   *R. Perkins*

'E' Class

Unit	Completed	Builder
Arun	1903	Cammell-Laird
Blackwater	1903	Cammell-Laird
Boyne	1904	Hawthorn
Chelmer	1904	Thornycroft
Cherwell	1903	Palmers
Colne	1905	Thornycroft
Dee	1905	Palmers
Derwent	1904	Hawthorn
Doon	1904	Hawthorn
Eden	1903	Hawthorn
Erne	1903	Palmers
Ettrick	1903	Palmers
Exe	1903	Palmers
Foyle	1903	Cammell-Laird
Gala	1905	Yarrow
Garry	1905	Yarrow
Itchen	1903	Cammell-Laird
Jed	1904	Thornycroft
Kale	1904	Hawthorn
Kennet	1903	Thornycroft
Liffey	1904	Cammell-Laird
Moy	1904	Cammell-Laird
Ness	1905	White
Nith	1905	White
Ouse	1905	Cammell-Laird
Ribble	1904	Yarrow
Rother	1904	Palmers
Stour	1909	Cammell-Laird
Swale	1905	Palmers
Test	1909	Cammell-Laird
Teviot	1903	Yarrow
Ure	1904	Palmers
Usk	1903	Yarrow
Waveney	1903	Hawthorn
Wear	1905	Palmers
Welland	1904	Yarrow

Displacement: 550 tons
Length: 225ft
Breadth: 23ft 6in
Draught: 10ft
Armament: *Main* Four 12pdr
Tubes Two 18in

Below: HMS *Derwent*, 'E' class, at sea 1898. *R. Perkins*

Bottom: HMS *Welland*, 'E' class, at anchor 1909. Note detail of transmitting/receiving aerials. *R. Perkins*

Machinery: Triple expansion on two shafts giving 7,000shp
Max speed: 25.5kts
Fuel: 120 tons coal

Class Notes

In this design can be seen the typical 'destroyer' hull outline with a raised forecastle. The ships of this class had either two or four funnels, the four funnels being in pairs. One of the tubes was sited aft and one on the centreline between the funnels.

HMS *Eden* had turbines with three screws on each of her two shafts.

HMS *Stour* and *Test* were powered by turbines.

Two ships of similar design named *Bonetta* and *Albacore* were constructed 1908-1910 to replace *Gala* and *Tiger*. These ships were of the following particulars: length 216ft, beam 21ft, mean draught 7ft 6in. They were powered by turbines of 6,000shp giving 27kts. They displaced 440 tons and had three 12-pounders and two 21in tubes. At 14kts they had approximately 2,000 miles radius. They were both coal fired.

Historical Notes

HMS *Derwent* struck a mine off le Harve on 2 May 1917.

HMS *Eden* sank after collision with the ss *France* in the English Channel on 17 June 1916.

HMS *Erne* was wrecked off Rattray Head near Aberdeen on 6 February 1915.

HMS *Foyle* struck a mine in the Straits of Dover on 15 March 1917.

HMS *Gala* and HMS *Tiger* sank after collision in 1908 (see Appendix 4).

HMS *Itchen* was torpedoed by a U-boat on 6 July 1917 in the North Sea.

HMS *Kale* struck a mine in the North Sea on 27 March 1918.

'F' Class

Unit	Completed	Builder
Afridi	1907	Vickers Armstrong (Tyne)
Amazon	1908	Thornycroft
Cossack	1907	Cammell-Laird
Crusader	1909	White
Ghurka	1907	Hawthorn
Maori	1909	Denny
Mohawk	1907	White
Nubian	1909	Thornycroft
Saracen	1908	White
Tartar	1907	Thornycroft
Viking	1909	Palmers
Zulu	1909	Hawthorn

Displacement: 870-970 tons
Length: 250-290ft
Breadth: 26ft
Draught: 9ft
Armament: *Main* Two 4in or Five 12pdr
Tubes Two 18in
Machinery: Turbines on two/three shafts giving 14,000-15,500shp

Max speed: 35kts
Fuel: 80-100 tons oil

Class Notes

All 12 of these vessels were different. Their funnels varied in number from three to six. (HMS *Viking* was the ship with six in three pairs of two.) This class saw the introduction of heavier armament on certain ships together with an increase of speed of over five knots on all earlier torpedo boat destroyers.

Historical Notes

The Dover Patrol was well served by this class and the well-known case of 'ship surgery' was performed on the battle-scarred fore part of *Zulu* and the after part of *Nubian*. The renaming question was solved by giving the joined portions which now made up a new destroyer the name of *Zubian*.

Below: HMS *Amazon*, 'F' class, at anchor 1911. Note small shield on A gun. *R. Perkins*

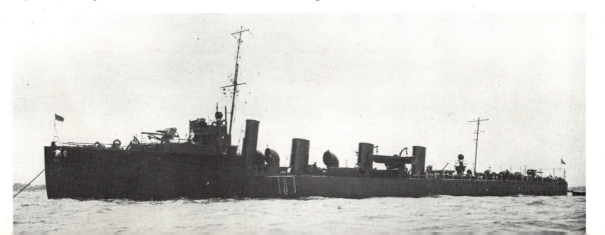

HMS *Ghurka* struck a mine on 8 February 1917 four miles south-east of Dungeness Buoy.

HMS *Maori* struck a mine two miles north-west of Wirlingen Light Ship near Zeebrugge on 7 May 1915.

HMS *Nubian* was torpedoed by German destroyers on 27 October 1916 whilst in action off Folkestone, but was towed into port.

Above: HMS *Cossack*, 'F' class, at anchor 1911. *R. Perkins*

HMS *Zulu* struck a mine on 27 October 1916 but was towed back into port.

'Swift' Class

Unit: *Swift*
Completed: 1907
Builder: Cammell-Laird
Displacement: 1,825 tons
2,207 tons full load
Length: 353ft
Breadth: 34ft 6in
Draught: 10ft 6in
Armament: *Main* Four 4in guns
Secondary One 2pdr
Tubes Two 18in
Machinery: Turbines on four shafts giving 30,000shp
Max speed: 36kts
Fuel: 180 tons oil

Class Notes
HMS *Swift* was a prototype for a class of ocean-going destroyers but she remained the only one of this design.

She had three large circular raked funnels and during builder's trials she attained the speed of 39kts.

Historical Notes
HMS *Swift* served as a leader during her time in the Dover Patrol 1914-18. After modernisation she mounted one 6in gun on the forecastle in place of the two forward 4in and her 18in tubes were changed to 21in. The 4in guns were the equivalent of 25-pounders. HMS *Swift* is the only destroyer in the Royal Navy ever to have mounted a 6in calibre gun and she was not approached in size until 1937.

Below: HMS *Swift* at speed trials 1919 during World War 1 with her new 6in gun in A position. *R. Perkins*

'G' Class

Unit	Completed	Builder
Basilisk	1910	White
Beagle	1909	Clydebank
Bulldog	1909	Clydebank
Foxhound	1909	Clydebank
Grampus (ex-*Nautilus*)	1910	Thames Iron Works
Grasshopper	1909	Fairfield
Harpy	1909	White
Mosquito	1910	Fairfield
Pincher	1910	Denny
Racoon	1910	Cammell-Laird
Rattlesnake	1910	Harland & Wolff (Clyde)
Renard	1909	Cammell-Laird
Savage	1910	Thornycroft
Scorpion	1910	Fairfield
Scourge	1910	Hawthorn
Wolverine	1910	Cammell-laird

Displacement: 860-940 tons
Length: 275ft
Breadth: 28ft
Draught: 8.5ft
Armament: *Main* One 4in

Secondary Three 12pdr
Tubes Two 21in
Machinery: Turbine on two/three shafts giving 12,500shp
Max speed: 27kts
Fuel: 120 tons coal

Class Notes

The ships of this class were all more or less uniform in appearance. The 4in was mounted on its own shelter deck where it was able to be fought in short, steep seas, being on a drier deck. The bridge was improved being more square and higher. One tube was just forward of the main mast, and the other positioned on the stern.

These ships were coal burning, there apparently being concern over oil stocks in the event of war. A further point of interest is that with the exception of HMS *Swift* (qv) this was the first class to carry the 21in torpedo;

Below: HMS *Bulldog*, 'G' class, 1910. Note A gun on raised deckhouse. *R. Perkins*

Bottom: HMS *Savage*, 'G' class at sea 1911. *R. Perkins*

additionally, this was the last destroyer class built for the Royal Navy to be coal fuelled.

Historical Notes
HMS *Pincher* was wrecked on the Seven Stones on 24 July 1918.

HMS *Racoon* was wrecked on 4 January 1918 on the Irish Coast in a snowstorm.

HMS *Wolverine* was sunk after collision with HMS *Rosemary* (sloop) on 12 December 1917 of Lough Foyle.

'H' Class

Unit	Completed	Builder	Unit	Completed	Builder
Acorn	1910	Clydebank	*Nymphe*	1911	Hawthorn
Alarm	1910	Clydebank	*Redpole*	1910	White
Brisk	1910	Clydebank	*Rifleman*	1910	White
Chameleon	1910	Fairfield	*Ruby*	1910	White
Comet	1910	Fairfield	*Sheldrake*	1911	Denny
Fury	1911	Inglis	*Staunch*	1910	Denny
Goldfinch	1910	Fairfield			
Hope	1910	Swan Hunter			
Larne	1910	Thornycroft			
Lyra	1910	Thornycroft			
Martin	1910	Thornycroft			
Minstrel	1911	Thornycroft			
Nemesis	1910	Hawthorn			
Nereide	1910	Hawthorn			

Displacement: 730-780 tons
Length: 246ft 6in
Breadth: 25ft 6in

Below: HMS *Chameleon*, 'H' class, at sea 1911. *R. Perkins*

Bottom: HMS *Rifleman*, 'H' class, entering harbour 1911. *R. Perkins*

Draught: 7-10ft
Armament: *Main* Two 4in
Secondary Two 12pdr
AA One 3pdr (in some)
Tubes Two 21in
Machinery: Turbines on three shafts giving 13,500shp
Max speed: 27kts
Fuel: 170 tons fuel oil

Class Notes

These ships had one tall funnel abaft the foremast, and two shorter and broader ones further aft spaced apart. The first tube was on the centreline between the second and third funnels. One 4in was in position A and one in Y with the 12-pounders on either beam at the break of the forecastle.

Historical Notes

HMS *Comet* was torpedoed 6 August 1918 by a U-boat in the Mediterranean.

HMS *Goldfinch* was wrecked on the night of 18/19 February 1915 in fog, at Start Point, Sanday Island, Orkneys.

HMS *Minstrel* and *Nemesis* were loaned to the Imperial Japanese Navy from 1917-18 and named HIM *Sendan* and *Kandan*.

HMS *Staunch* was torpedoed on 11 November 1917, by a U-boat off Gaza, Palestine.

'I' Class

Unit	Completed	Builder
Acheron	1911	Thornycroft
Archer	1911	Yarrow
Ariel	1911	Thornycroft
Attack	1911	Yarrow
Badger	1911	Hawthorn
Beaver	1911	Hawthorn
Defender	1911	Denny
Druid	1911	Denny
Ferret	1911	White
Firedrake	1912	Yarrow
Forester	1911	White
Goshawk	1911	Beardmore
Hind	1911	Clydebank
Hornet	1911	Clydebank
Hydra	1912	Clydebank
Jackal	1911	Hawthorn
Lapwing	1911	Cammell-Laird
Lizard	1911	Cammell-Laird
Lurcher	1912	Yarrow
Oak	1912	Yarrow
Phoenix	1911	Vickers Armstrong (Barrow)
Sandfly	1911	Swan Hunter
Tigress	1911	Hawthorn

[handwritten annotations: "White → Forster", "2 screws Brown Curtis", "Yarrow", "ADMIRALTY"]

Displacement: 750-790 tons
Length: 246ft (*Acheron* 252ft)
Breadth: 26ft 9in (*Acheron* 26ft)
Draught: 8ft 6in (*Acheron* 9ft)
Armament: *Main* Two 4in
Secondary two 12 pdr
AA One 3pdr
Tubes Two 21in
Machinery: Turbines on two shafts giving 16,500-20,000shp
Max speed: 30-32kts
Fuel: 150-180 tons oil

Class Notes

Originally only 20 of this class were built but *Lurcher*, *Firedrake* and *Oak* brought the total to 23 after three ships were transferred to the Royal Australian Navy. All ships had two funnels of the same height with the exception of the latter three. Guns were mounted as in the 'H' class.

Below: HMS *Archer*, 'I' class, at sea 1912. *R. Perkins*

HMS *Archer* and *Attack* used steam at a higher temperature being superheated, and HMS *Badger* and *Beaver* were completed with geared turbines for trials.

Above: HMS *Lapwing*, 'I' class, 1913. Note main mast is vertical under strain from aerials, and the bands on the funnel denoting flotilla leader. *R. Perkins*

Historical Notes

HMS *Ariel* struck a mine whilst minelaying on 2 August 1918 in the North Sea.

HMS *Attack* was torpedoed by a U-boat on 30 December 1917 off Alexandria.

HMS *Phoenix* was torpedoed by a U-boat on 14 May 1918 in the Adriatic.

'K' Class

Unit	Completed	Builder
Acasta	1912	Clydebank
Achates	1912	Clydebank
Ambuscade	1913	Clydebank
Ardent	1913	Denny
Christopher	1912	Hawthorn
Cockatrice	1912	Hawthorn
Contest	1913	Hawthorn
Fortune	1913	Fairfield
Garland	1913	Cammell-Laird
Hardy	1912	Thornycroft
Lynx	1912	Harland & Wolff
Midge	1912	Harland & Wolff
Owl	1912	Harland & Wolff
Paragon	1913	Thornycroft
Porpoise	1913	Thornycroft
Shark	1912	Swan Hunter
Sparrowhawk	1912	Swan Hunter
Spitfire	1913	Swan Hunter
Unity	1913	Thornycroft
Victor	1913	Thornycroft

Displacement: 934-984 tons
Length: 267ft 6in
Breadth: 27ft
Draught: 9ft 6in (*Hardy* 8ft)
Armament: *Main* Three 4in
AA One 2pdr
Tubes Two 21in (single mountings)
Machinery: Turbines on two/three shafts giving 22,500-25,000shp
Max speed: 31kts
Fuel: 160-200 tons oil

Class Notes

These ships had three funnels, all being circular, the first the tallest. The 4in guns were mounted in A position, on either beam of the second tube, or one before and one after the second tube. This was the last class to have mixed names. All following began with the same letter, subject to suitability.

HMS *Hardy* was fitted with a diesel engine for cruising.

HMS *Fortune* although of this class in superstructure was actually the prototype hull of the 'L' class, with a clipper bow.

Historical Notes

HMS *Ardent* was sunk by gunfire from ships of the German High Seas Fleet in the Battle of Jutland on 1 June 1916.

HMS *Contest* was sunk by a U-boat on 18 September 1917.

HMS *Fortune* was hit and sunk by gunfire by ships of the German High Seas Fleet in the Battle of Jutland sinking about midnight 31 May/1 June 1916.

HMS *Lynx* struck a mine 9 August 1915 in the Moray Firth.

HMS *Paragon* was torpedoed in action in the Straits of Dover, 18 March 1917, by a German destroyer.

HMS *Shark* was torpedoed after being hit by German light cruisers' gunfire in the Battle of Jutland 31 May 1916.

HMS *Sparrowhawk* was disabled during the Battle of Jutland after collision with HMS *Broke* and to avoid falling into enemy hands was torpedoed by HMS *Marksman* on 1 June 1916.

Below: HMS *Midge* 'K' class, at sea, 1914. *R. Perkins*

Bottom: HMS *Porpoise*, 'K' class, at sea, 1914. *R. Perkins*

'L' Class

Unit	Completed	Builder	Unit	Completed	Builder
Laertes	1913	Swan Hunter	*Lawford*	1913	Fairfield
Laforey	1913	Fairfield	*Legion*	1914	Denny
Lance	1914	Thornycroft	*Lennox*	1914	Beardmore
Landrail	1914	Yarrow	*Leonidas*	1913	Hawthorn
Lark	1913	Yarrow	*Liberty*	1913	White
Lassoo	1915	Beardmore	*Linnet*	1913	Yarrow
Laurel	1913	White	*Llewellyn*	1913	Beardmore
Laverock	1914	Yarrow	*Lochinvar*	1915	Beardmore

Unit	Completed	Builder
Lookout	1914	Thornycroft
Louis	1913	Fairfield
Loyal	1913	Denny
Lucifer	1913	Hawthorn
Lydiard	1914	Hawthorn
Lysander	1913	Swan Hunter

Displacement: 965-1,003 tons
Length: 269ft
Breadth: 26ft 9in
Draught: 9ft 6in
Armament: *Main* Three 4in
AA One 2pdr
Tubes Four 21in (2 × 2)
Machinery: Turbine on two shafts giving 24,500shp
(22,500shp *Leonidas* and *Lucifer*)
Max speed: 29kts
Fuel: 200-290 tons oil

Class Notes

Of this class 16 ships had three funnels with the centre
one broader than the other two, the remaining six ships
having two funnels only. A searchlight was positioned
between the tube mountings which were aft of the funnels.
In the three-funnelled ships the second 4in gun was
positioned between the second and third funnels upon a
'bandstand'.

All these vessels were allocated 'L' names, but each had been
given a different name beforehand. In order listed these
were: *Sarpedon; Florizel; Daring; Hotspur; Haughty;
Magic; Redgauntlet; Hereward; Ivanhoe; Viola; Portia;
Rob Roy; Rosalind; Havock; Picton; Malice; Dragon;
Talisman; Orlando; Rocket; Waverley; Ulysses.*

Historical Notes

HMS *Laforey* and *Leonidas* were the first torpedo boat
destroyers to have geared turbines.

HMS *Laforey* struck a mine and sank in the English
Channel on 23 March 1917.

HMS *Lance* is reputed to have fired the first shot of
World War I.

HMS *Lassoo* was torpedoed off the Maas Light Ship on
13 August 1916 by a German U-boat.

HMS *Legion* was equipped for minelaying.

HMS *Louis* was wrecked on 31 October 1915 in Suvla
Bay.

Below: HMS *Legion*, 'L' class, at sea, 1914.   *R. Perkins*

Bottom: HMS *Linnet*, 'L' class, standing by for sunset, 1914.   *R. Perkins*

Admiralty 'M' Class

Unit	Completed	Builder	Unit	Completed	Builder
Maenad	1915	Denny	*Nonpareil*	1916	Stephen (Completed by Beardmore)
Magic (ex-*Marigold*)	1916	White			
Mameluke	1915	Clydebank	*Nonsuch* (ex-*Narcissus*)	1916	Palmers
Mandate	1915	Fairfield	*Norman*	1916	Palmers
Manners	1915	Fairfield	*Norseman*	1916	Doxford
Marmion	1915	Swan Hunter	*Northesk*	1916	Palmers
Marne	1915	Clydebank	*North Star*	1917	Palmers
Martial	1915	Swan Hunter	*Nugent*	1917	Palmers
Marvel	1915	Denny	*Obdurate*	1916	Scotts
Mary Rose	1916	Palmers	*Obedient*	1916	Scotts
Matchless	1914	Swan Hunter	*Oberon*	1916	Doxford
Medina (ex-*Redmill*)	1916	White	*Observer*	1916	Fairfield
Medway (ex-*Redwing*)	1916	White	*Octavia* (ex-*Onyx*)	1916	Doxford
Menace	1916	Swan Hunter	*Offa*	1916	Fairfield
Michael	1915	Thornycroft	*Onslaught*	1916	Fairfield
Millbrook	1915	Thornycroft	*Onslow*	1916	Fairfield
Milne	1914	Clydebank	*Opal*	1916	Doxford
Mindful	1915	Fairfield	*Ophelia*	1916	Doxford
Minion	1915	Thornycroft	*Opportune*	1916	Doxford
Mischief	1915	Fairfield	*Oracle*	1916	Doxford
Mons	1915	Clydebank	*Orcadia*	1916	Fairfield
Moorsom	1915	Clydebank	*Orestes*	1916	Doxford
Moresby (ex-*Marlion*)	1916	White	*Orford*	1916	Doxford
Morris	1914	Clydebank	*Oriana*	1916	Fairfield
Munster (ex-*Monitor*)	1916	Thornycroft	*Oriole*	1916	Palmers
Murray	1914	Palmers	*Orpheus*	1916	Doxford
Myngs	1915	Palmers	*Osiris*	1916	Palmers
Mystic (ex-*Myrtle*)	1915	Denny	*Ossory*	1916	Clydebank
Napier	1916	Clydebank	*Paladin*	1916	Scotts
Narborough	1916	Clydebank	*Parthian*	1916	Scotts
Narwhal	1916	Denny	*Partridge*	1916	Swan Hunter
Negro	1916	Palmers	*Pasley*	1916	Swan Hunter
Nepean	1916	Thornycroft	*Pelican*	1916	Beardmore
Nereus	1916	Thornycroft	*Pellew*	1916	Beardmore
Nessus	1915	Swan Hunter	*Penn*	1916	Clydebank
Nestor	1916	Swan Hunter			
Nicator	1916	Denny			
Nizam	1916	Stephen			
Noble (ex-*Nisus*)	1916	Stephen			
Nomad	1916	Stephen			

Below: HMS *Medina*, Admiralty 'M' class, in war colours, 1919. Note larger shield for A gun and pennant number. *R. Perkins*

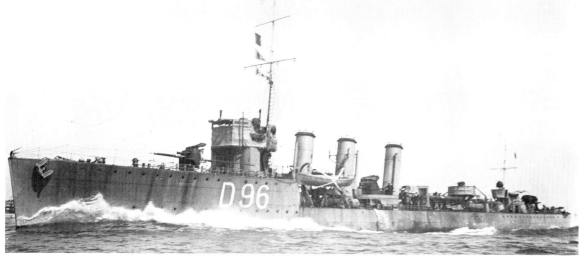

Unit	Completed	Builder
Peregrin	1916	Clydebank
Petard	1916	Denny
Peyton	1916	Denny
Pheasant	1916	Fairfield
Phoebe	1916	Fairfield
Pigeon	1916	Hawthorn
Plover	1916	Hawthorn
Plucky	1916	Scotts
Portia	1916	Scotts
Prince	1916	Stephen
Pylades	1916	Stephen

Displacement: 994-1,042 tons
Length: 269ft
Breadth: 27ft 6in
Draught: 10ft 6in
Armament: *Main* Three 4in
AA One 2pdr
Tubes Four 21in (2×2)
Machinery: Turbines on three shafts giving 25,000shp
Max speed: 34kts
Fuel: 300 tons oil

Class Notes

These were all three-funnelled ships, the funnels being of the same height, circular but narrow. Positioning of armament as for the 'L' class. A number of the earlier destroyers of this class had cruising turbines which were omitted from later buildings.

HMS *Partridge, Norman, Maenad, Ophelia* and *Observer* were fitted out to carry a kite balloon.

Historical Notes

HMS *Marmion* sank on 21 October 1917 after collision with HMS *Tirade* off the Shetlands.

HMS *Mary Rose* was sunk by gunfire from the German light cruisers SMS *Bremse* and *Brummer* on 17 October 1917 off the Norwegian coast in a convoy action.

HMS *Narborough* sank with HMS *Opal* in a storm on 12 January 1918 outside Scapa Flow.

HMS *Negro* sank on 21 December 1916 after collision with HMS *Hoste* in the North Sea during bad weather.

HMS *Nessus* sank after colliding with HMS *Amphitrite* on 8 September 1918 in bad weather in the North Sea.

HMS *Nestor* was sunk by gunfire from ships of the German High Seas Fleet on 31 May 1916 during the Battle of Jutland.

HMS *Nomad* was sunk by gunfire by the ships of the German High Seas Fleet on 31 May 1916.

HMS *North Star* was sunk at Zeebrugge by gunfire from German shore batteries on 23 April 1918.

HMS *Partridge* was sunk by gunfire on 12 December 1917 during an action with four German destroyers guarding a convoy off the Norwegian coast.

HMS *Pheasant* struck a mine and sank, 1 March 1917, off the Orkneys.

Hawthorn 'M' Class

Units: *Mansfield, Mentor*
Completed: 1915
Builder: Hawthorn-Leslie
Displacement: 1,057 tons
Length: 271ft
Breadth: 27ft 6in

Draught: 10ft 6in
Armament: *Main* Three 4in
AA One 2pdr
Tubes Four 21in (2×2)
Machinery: Turbines on three shafts giving 27,000shp
Max speed: 35kts

Fuel: 300 tons oil

Above: HMS *Mansfield*, Hawthorn 'M' class, at sea 1916. *IWM*

Class Notes

A Hawthorn derivative of the Admiralty 'M' design. The second 4in was situated aft of the second funnel and forward of the third. The funnels were in pairs. The tubes were in pairs and mounted on the centreline.

Yarrow 'M' Class

Unit	Completed
Manley	1914
Minos	1914
Miranda	1914
Moon	1915
Morning Star	1915
Mounsey	1915
Musketeer	1915
Nerissa	1916
Relentless	1916
Rival	1916

Builder: Yarrow
Displacement: 879-898 tons
Length: 271ft
Breadth: 27ft
Draught: 10ft 6in
Armament: *Main* Three 4in
AA One 2pdr

Tubes Four 21in (2×2)
Machinery: Turbine on two shafts giving 25,000-27,000shp
Max speed: 36kts
Fuel: 200-230 tons oil

Class Notes

All ships had two funnels, the foremost broader than the aft one. Apart from this they were similar to the Admiralty 'M' class of 1914. These ships had a straight stern.

HMS *Moon, Mounsey* and *Musketeer* were fitted out to carry a kite balloon.

Below: HMS *Minos*, Yarrow 'M' class, entering harbour 1914.
R. Perkins

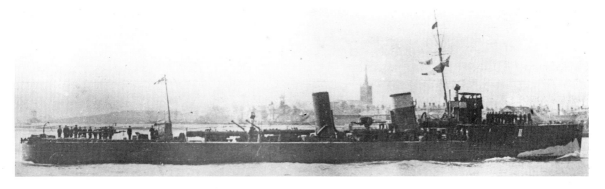

Above: HMS *Relentless*, Yarrow 'M' class, entering harbour 1914. *R. Perkins*

Thornycroft 'M' Class

Unit	Completed
Mastiff	1914
Meteor	1914
Patrician	1916
Patriot	1916
Rapid	1916
Ready	1916

Builder: Thornycroft
Displacement: 985-1,070 tons
Length: 274ft
Breadth: 27ft 6in
Draught: 10ft 6in
Armament: *Main* Three 4in
AA One 2pdr
Tubes Four 21in (2 × 2)

Machinery: Turbines on two shafts giving 25,000-27,000shp
Max speed: 35kts
Fuel: 300 tons oil

Class Notes
These ships were similar to those of the 'L' class of 1913 but all had three funnels. All of this class were a derivation of the Admiralty 'M' design of 1914 which were enlargements of the 'L' class.

HMS *Patriot* was fitted out to carry a kite balloon.

Below: HMS *Rapid*, Thornycroft 'M' class, leaving harbour 1924. Note enclosed after conning position. *R. Perkins*

Above: HMS *Ready*, Thornycroft 'M' class, at anchor 1918. *R. Perkins*

Ex-Turkish New Buildings

Units: *Talisman, Termagant, Trident, Turbulent*
Completed: 1916
Builder: Hawthorn-Leslie
Displacement: 1,098 tons
Length: 309ft
Breadth: 28ft 6in
Draught: 9ft 6in
Armament: *Main* Five 4in
Tubes Four 21in (2 × 2)
Machinery: Turbines on three shafts giving 25,000shp
Max speed: 32kts
Fuel: 238 tons oil

Class Notes
All of these ships frequently acted as leaders. The positioning of the 4in guns was rather peculiar: in A position on the forecastle two 4in guns were mounted side-by-side, a further 4in was mounted between the first pair of funnels, the fourth was aft of the tubes and the fifth 4in surmounting a 'bandstand' on the quarterdeck. They were very successful ships, seaworthy and the design proved to be the basis for the Admiralty 'V' and 'W' classes. Depth charges were carried.

Historical Notes
HMS *Turbulent* sank during the Battle of Jutland after colliding with a large unidentified German vessel on 31 May 1916.

Below: HMS *Trident* (ex-Turkish) at sea, 1916. *IWM*

Left: HMS *Talisman* (ex-Turkish) at sea, 1916. *IWM*

Ex-Greek New Buildings

Unit	Builder
Medea (ex-*Kriti*)	Clydebank
Medusa (ex-*Lesvos*)	Clydebank
Melampus (ex-*Chios*)	Fairfield
Melpomene (ex-*Samos*)	Fairfield

Completed: 1915
Displacement: 1,040 tons
Length: 273ft 6in
Breadth: 26ft 6in
Draught: 10ft 6in
Armament: *Main* Three 4in
Tubes Four 21in (2 × 2)
Machinery: Turbines on three shafts giving 25,000shp

Max speed: 32kts
Fuel: 270 tons oil

Class notes
In these ships the foremast was shorter than the main and the fore funnel taller than the second and third.

Historical Notes
HMS *Medusa* was lost in a collision on the 25 March 1916 with HMS *Laverock* off the Schlieswig Coast.

Below: HMS *Melampus* (ex-Greek) at sea, 1914.   *R. Perkins*

Ex-Chilean New Buildings

Units: *Tipperary* (ex-*Almirante Riveres*), *Botha* (ex-*Almirante Williams Rebelledo*), *Broke* (ex-*Almirante Goni*), *Faulknor* (ex-*Almirante Simpson*)
Completed: 1914 (*Tipperary* 1915)
Builders: White

Displacement: 1,700-1,850 tons average
Length: 331ft 6in

Below: HMS *Broke* (ex-Chilean) 1914. Note two single guns in A position abeam of the bridge and on the stern.   *R. Perkins*

Breadth: 32ft 6in
Draught: 11ft
Armament: *Main* Two 4.7in
Secondary Two 4in
AA Two 2pdr
Tubes Four 21in (2 × 2)
Machinery: Turbines on three shafts giving 30,000shp
Max speed: 32kts
Fuel: 403 tons coal
83 tons oil

Class Notes
All these ships had four funnels, the first tall and narrow, the other three being equally spaced but shorter. The ships of this class were rated as leaders. HMS *Botha* had tubes in single mountings. All ships of this class originally had four 4in and two 2pdr AA guns.

Historical Notes
HMS *Tipperary* was sunk by gunfire from ships of the German High Seas Fleet at the Battle of Jutland 31 May 1916.

'Marksman' Class

Unit	Completed	Builder
Abdiel	1916	Cammell-Laird
Gabriel	1916	Cammell-Laird
Ithuriel	1916	Cammell-Laird
Kempenfelt	1915	Cammell-Laird
Lightfoot	1915	White
Marksman	1915	Hawthorn-Leslie
Nimrod	1915	Denny

Displacement: 1,600 tons average
Length: 321ft
Breadth: 31ft 9in
Draught: 11ft
Armament: *Main* Four 4in
AA Two 2pdr

Tubes Four 21in (2 × 2)
Machinery: Turbines on three shafts giving 36,000shp
Max speed: 34kts
Fuel: 510 tons oil

Class Notes
All were four-funnelled ships, the first funnel being taller than the others. The guns were in A position and between the first, second and third funnels. HMS *Abdiel* was a minelayer with no stern gun or tubes and all funnels of equal height. She was armed with three 4in guns, and was screened from the fourth funnel to the stern on the main deck to give shelter for 60-70 mines.

HMS *Gabriel* was also later fitted out as a minelayer and carried 72 mines.

Above left: HMS *Abdiel*, 'Marksman' class, flying pennant number, 1926. *R. Perkins*

Left: HMS *Nimrod*, 'Marksman' class, 1924 flying pennant number with unusual pattern of aerial. *R. Perkins*

'Anzac' Class

Units: *Anzac, Grenville, Hoste, Parker* (ex-*Frobisher*), *Saumarez, Seymour*
Completed: 1916 (*Anzac* 1917)
Builder: Cammell-Laird (*Anzac* Denny)
Displacement: 1,670 tons
Length: 325ft
Breadth: 31ft 9in
Draught: 10ft 6in
Armament: *Main* four 4in (director controlled)
Secondary Two 2pdr
AA One 3in
Tubes Four 21in (2 × 2)
Machinery: Turbine on three shafts giving 36,000shp
Max speed: 34kts
Fuel: 415 tons oil

Class Notes

These were all three-funnelled ships — the first funnel being taller and thicker than any of the others. Two of the 4in guns were positioned on the fore deck in A and B position, superimposed. These ships were built as leaders.

Historical Notes

HMS *Anzac* was presented to the Government of Australia for use by the RAN in 1919.

HMS *Hoste* was lost after a collision on 21 December 1916 in the North Sea.

Below: HMS *Saumarez*, 'Anzac' class, 1919. Note A and B guns superimposed. *R. Perkins*

Bottom: HMS *Anzac*, 'Anzac' class, 1919. Note A and B guns superimposed. *R. Perkins*

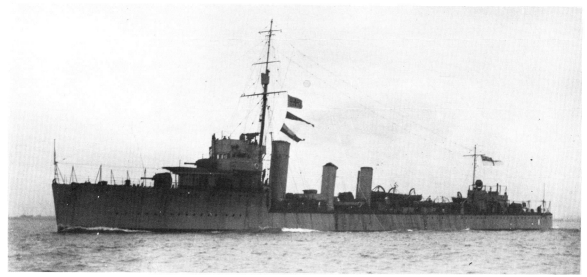

'Arno' Class

Unit: *Arno* (ex-*Liz*)
Commenced: 1914
Completed: 1915
Builders: Ansaldo (Genoa)
Displacement: 520 tons
Length: 321ft
Breadth: 23ft 6in
Draught: 7ft
Armament: *Main* Four 3in (12pdr)
Tubes Three 18in (1×3)
Machinery: Turbines on two shafts giving 8,000shp
Max speed: 28.5kts
Fuel: 130 tons oil

Class Notes

This destroyer was purchased whilst still building from the Portuguese government, such was the British need for destroyer tonnage at that time. The two forward 3in guns were positioned on the fore deck in A position close to the base of the tall bridge. The third 3in gun was positioned at the rear of the funnel and the fourth 3in was positioned on the stern.

HMS *Arno* was quite a good-looking ship with straight stem and two funnels and inward sloping topsides towards the stern. Although smaller than the conventional British destroyer of the time, she was a well-built ship with a number of good features including high freeboard and tall protective bridge.

Historical Notes

HMS *Arno* was lost by collision with HMS *Hope* (destroyer) in the Dardanelles on 23 March 1918.

Below: HMS *Arno* (ex-Portuguese) leaving Grand Harbour Valetta, 1916. *IWM*

Admiralty 'R' Class

Unit	Completed	Builder	Unit	Completed	Builder
Radstock	1916	Swan Hunter	*Setter*	1917	Beardmore
Raider	1916	Swan Hunter	*Sharpshooter*	1917	Beardmore
Recruit	1917	Doxford	*Simoon*	1916	Clydebank
Redgauntlet	1917	Denny	*Skate*	1917	Clydebank
Redoubt	1917	Doxford	*Skilful*	1917	Harland & Wolff
Restless	1916	Clydebank	*Sorceress*	1916	Swan Hunter
Rigorous	1916	Clydebank	*Springbok*	1917	Harland & Wolff
Rob Roy	1916	Denny	*Starfish*	1916	Hawthorn
Rocket	1916	Denny	*Stork*	1917	Hawthorn
Romola	1916	Clydebank	*Sturgeon*	1917	Stephen
Rowena	1916	Clydebank	*Sylph*	1917	Harland & Wolff
Sable	1916	White	*Tancred*	1917	Beardmore
Salmon	1916	Harland & Wolff	*Tarpon*	1917	Clydebank
Sarpedon	1916	Hawthorn	*Telemachus*	1917	Clydebank
Satyr	1917	Beardmore	*Tempest*	1917	Fairfield
Sceptre	1917	Stephen	*Tenacious*	1917	Harland & Wolff

Unit	Completed	Builder
Tetrarch	1917	Harland & Wolff
Thisbe	1917	Hawthorn
Thruster	1917	Hawthorn
Tormentor	1917	Stephen
Tornado	1917	Stephen
Torrent	1917	Swan Hunter
Torrid	1917	Swan Hunter

Displacement: 1,040 tons
Length: 276ft
Breadth: 26ft 9in
Draught: 10ft 6in
Armament: *Main* Three 4in
AA One 2pdr, One MG
Tubes Four 21in (2×2)
Machinery: Geared turbines on two shafts giving 27,000shp
Max speed: 36kts
Fuel: 285-300 tons oil

Class Notes

These ships were similar to the Admiralty 'M' class in appearance, the difference being the after 4in gun in a bandstand and the curved sloping stern.

Historical Notes

HMS *Recruit* sank after striking a mine on 9 August 1917 in the North Sea.

HMS *Salmon* was renamed *Sable* in 1933, and HMS *Sable* was renamed HMS *Salmon* in the same year.

HMS *Setter* sank after colliding with HMS *Sylph* in fog off Harwich on 17 May 1917.

HMS *Simoon* was sunk by gunfire from German destroyers off Schouwen Bank on 23 January 1917.

HMS *Tarpon* and *Telemachus* were fitted out as minelayers.

HMS *Tornado* and *Torrent* were torpedoed and sunk by a German U-boat on the night of 22/23 December 1917 off the Maas Light Ship.

Below: HMS *Skate*, Admiralty 'R' class, 1917. Note symmetrical fore and main masts.

Bottom: HMS *Tarpon*, Admiralty 'R' class, 1924. Note larger gun shield on A gun and minelaying rails at the stern. *R. Perkins*

Yarrow Later 'M' Class

Unit	Completed
Sabrina	1916
Strongbow	1916
Surprise	1916
Sybille	1917
Truculent	1917
Tyrant	1917
Ulleswater	1917

Builder: Yarrow
Displacement: 897-923 tons
Length: 271ft 6in
Breadth: 25ft 9in
Draught: 10ft 6in
Armament: *Main* three 4in
Secondary One 2pdr
Tubes Four 21in (2×2)
Machinery: Turbines on two shafts giving 27,000shp
Max speed: 36kts
Fuel: 215-260 tons oil

Class Notes

All these ships had a likeness to their predecessors, the earlier Yarrow 'M' class; they were, however, of narrower beam, greater tonnage and had sloping sterns.

Historical Notes

HMS *Strongbow* was sunk by gunfire from the German light cruisers SMS *Bremse* and *Brummer* off the Norwegian coast in a convoy action on 17 October 1917.

HMS *Surprise* was torpedoed by a German U-boat off the Maas Light Ship on the night of 22/23 December 1917.

HMS *Ulleswater* was torpedoed by a German U-boat (*UC-17*) off the Dutch coast on 15 August 1918.

Below: HMS *Truculent*, Yarrow later 'M' class, at sea 1924. *R. Perkins*

Bottom: HMS *Tyrant*, Yarrow later 'M' class, at sea 1924. *R. Perkins*

Thornycroft 'R' Class

Units: *Radiant, Retriever, Rosalind, Taurus, Teazer*
Completed: 1917 (*Rosalind* 1916)
Builder: Thornycroft
Displacement: 1,034-1,064 tons
Length: 274ft
Breadth: 27ft
Draught: 11ft
Armament: *Main* Three 4in
Secondary One 2pdr
Tubes Four 21in (2×2)
AS 30 300lb DCs carried
Machinery: Turbines on two shafts giving 29,000shp
Max speed: 35kts
Fuel: 285-320 tons oil

Class Notes

These ships were similar to the 'M' class built by Thornycroft in 1914, the main difference being that the after 4in was on a 'bandstand'. All ships of this class had three funnels, the second funnel being broader than the first and third, all raked and capped. On trials HMS *Teazer* is said to have exceeded 40kts and all others of this class surpassed their contract speed. The 4in guns of this and previous classes had an elevation of 20°.

HMS *Radiant* later became the *Phra Ruang* of the Royal Siamese Navy.

Below: HMS *Radiant*, Thornycroft 'R' class, at anchor 1918.
R. Perkins

Bottom: HMS *Rosalind*, Thornycroft 'R' class, at anchor 1918.
R. Perkins

Admiralty Modified 'R' Class

Unit	Builder
Tirade	Scotts
Tower	Swan Hunter
Trenchant	White
Tristram	White
Ulster	Beardmore
Ulysses	Doxford
Umpire	Doxford
Undine	Fairfield
Urchin	Palmers
Ursa	Palmers
Ursula	Scotts

Completed: 1917
Displacement: 1,085 tons
Length: 276ft
Breadth: 26ft 9in
Draught: 11ft
Armament: *Main* Three 4in
Secondary One 2pdr
Tubes Four 21in (2×2)
Machinery: Geared turbines on two shafts giving 27,000shp
Max speed: 36kts
Fuel: 280 tons oil

Class Notes

This class was a combination of the designs of two previous classes — the Yarrow 'M' and the Admirality 'R'. The ships had two funnels, the aftermost being of lesser diameter and the bridge structure was also higher. Above the second pair of tubes was a searchlight which trained with them. The after 4in gun was in X position on a 'bandstand'. HMS *Ulster* and *Ursa* had 30° elevation on the main 4in armament.

Historical Notes

HMS *Ulysses* sank after a collision with SS *Ellerie* (merchant ship) in the Firth of Clyde on 29 October 1918. She was the last destroyer to be lost in World War I.

Below: HMS *Trenchant*, Admiralty modified 'R' class, 1924. Note ribs on forefunnel. *R. Perkins*

Bottom: HMS *Umpire*, Admiralty modified 'R' class, at anchor 1918. *R. Perkins*

Admiralty 'S' Class

Unit	Completed	Builder	Unit	Completed	Builder
Sabre	1918	Stephen	*Splendid*	1918	Swan Hunter
Saladin	1919	Stephen	*Sportive*	1918	Swan Hunter
Sardonyx	1919	Stephen	*Stalwart*	1919	Swan Hunter
Scimitar	1918	Clydebank	*Steadfast*	1919	Palmers
Scotsman	1918	Clydebank	*Sterling*	1919	Palmers
Scout	1918	Clydebank	*Stonehenge*	1919	Palmers
Scythe	1918	Clydebank	*Stormcloud*	1919	Palmers
Seabear	1918	Clydebank	*Strenuous*	1919	Scotts
Seafire	1918	Clydebank	*Stronghold*	1919	Scotts
Searcher	1918	Clydebank	*Sturdy*	1919	Scotts
Seawolf	1919	Clydebank	*Success*	1919	Doxford
Senator	1918	Denny	*Swallow*	1918	Scotts
Sepoy	1918	Denny	*Swordsman*	1918	Scotts
Seraph	1918	Denny	*Tactician*	1918	Beardmore
Serapis	1919	Denny	*Tara*	1918	Beardmore
Serene	1919	Denny	*Tasmania*	1919	Beardmore
Sesame	1919	Denny	*Tattoo*	1919	Beardmore
Shamrock	1919	Doxford	*Tenedos*	1919	Hawthorn
Shark	1918	Swan Hunter	*Thanet*	1919	Hawthorn
Shikari	1924	Doxford, completed by HM Dockyard Chatham	*Thracian*	1922	Hawthorn, completed by HM Dockyard Chatham
Sikh	1918	Fairfield			
Simoon	1918	Clydebank			
Sirdar	1918	Fairfield			
Somme	1918	Fairfield			
Sparrowhawk	1918	Swan Hunter			
Spear	1918	Fairfield			
Spindrift	1919	Fairfield			

Below: HMS *Shikari*, Admiralty 'S' class, at sea 1925. *R. Perkins*

Bottom: HMS *Tilbury*, Admiralty 'S' class, entering harbour 1925. *R. Perkins*

Unit	Completed	Builder
Tilbury	1918	Swan Hunter
Tintagel	1918	Swan Hunter
Tribune	1918	White
Trinidad	1918	White
Trojan	1919	White
Truant	1919	White
Trusty	1919	White
Turbulent	1919	Hawthorn

Displacement: 1,075 tons
Length: 276ft
Breadth: 26ft 9in
Draught: 10ft 6in
Armament: *Main* Three 4in
Secondary One 2pdr
Tubes Four 21in (2×2)
Two 14in either beam at break of foc'sle (2×1)
AS 30 DCs carried.
Machinery: Turbines on two shafts giving 27,000shp
Max speed: 36kts
Fuel: 250-300 tons oil

Class Notes
This was a coastal design for the North Sea and English Channel; they did, however, travel to far distant seas. They had a long foc'sle and tall bridge. The majority of this class had one 14in tube fixed at the break of the foc'sle to be launched abeam in night actions. All had two funnels, the foremost broader and taller than the second and both were raked.

Historical Notes
HMS *Shikari* on commissioning was the control vessel for the target ships *Agamemnon* and *Centurion*.

HMS *Stalwart, Success, Swordsman, Tattoo* and *Tasmania* were transferred to the Royal Australian Navy in 1918.

HMS *Sterling* was so named due to a typing error; her intended name was *Stirling*.

HMS *Stronghold* on 2 March 1942 was sunk by a Japanese Task Force off the east coast of Malaya.

HMS *Sturdy* was wrecked in bad weather on 30 October 1940, off the Island of Tiree, West Scotland.

HMS *Tenedos* was sunk after Japanese aircraft attack on Colombo Roads on 5 April 1942.

Between 1923 and 1928, both HMS *Thanet* and *Stronghold* were fitted with aircraft catapults on the foc'sle.

HMS *Thanet* was sunk by the Japanese on 28 January 1942 off the east coast of Malaya.

HMS *Thracian* was taken by the Japanese whilst beached at Hong Kong in 1942, but was recovered in 1945 and sold in 1947.

Yarrow 'S' Class

Unit	Completed
Tomahawk	1918
Torch	1918
Tryphon	1918
Tumult	1918
Turquoise	1919
Tuscan	1919
Tyrian	1919

Builder: Yarrow
Displacement: 930 tons
Length: 269ft 6in
Breadth: 25ft 9in
Draught: 11ft
Armament: *Main* Three 4in with 30° elevation
AA One 2pdr
Tubes Four 21in (2×2)
AS 30 DCs carried
Machinery: Turbines on two shafts giving 23,000shp
Max speed: 36kts
Fuel: 215-255 tons oil

Class Notes
The characteristics of these ships were as for the Admiralty 'S' class, except that they had a sloping stern, and a broader fore funnel.

Below: HMS *Tuscan*, Yarrow 'S' class leaving harbour, 1920.
R. Perkins

Historical Notes

HMS *Tryphon* grounded off Tenedos on 6 May 1919 but was salvaged and refitted.

Above: HMS *Tyrian*, Yarrow 'S' class at anchor 1925. *R. Perkins*

Thornycroft 'S' Class

Unit	Completed
Speedy	1918
Tobago	1918
Torbay	1919
Toreador	1919
Tourmaline	1919

Builder: Thornycroft
Displacement: 1,087 tons
Length: 275ft 9in
Breadth: 27ft 6in

Draught: 10ft
Armament: *Main* Three 4in with 30° elevation
AA Two 2pdr
Tubes Four 21in (2×2)
AS 30 DCs carried
Machinery: Geared turbines on two shafts giving 29,000shp

Below: HMS *Toreador*, Thornycroft 'S' class, entering harbour 1920. *R. Perkins*

44

Max speed: 36kts
Fuel: 250-300 tons oil

Above: HMS *Tourmaline*, Thornycroft 'S' class, at sea. *R. Perkins*

Class Notes

This class had a greater freeboard than the Yarrow and Admiralty 'S' classes and had two funnels of equal height, taller than the 'S' class. The A gun was mounted on a short shelter deck.

Historical Notes

HMS *Tobago*, although not strictly a war loss, was nevertheless a victim of a weapon of war, being mined whilst on patrol in the Black Sea in 1920.

Admiralty 'V' Class

Unit	Completed	Builder	Unit	Completed	Builder
Valentine (leader)	1917	Cammell-Laird	*Venturous*	1917	Denny
Valhalla (leader)	1917	Cammell-Laird	*Verdun*	1917	Hawthorn
Valkyrie (leader)	1917	Denny	*Versatile*	1918	Hawthorn
Valorous (leader)	1917	Denny	*Verulam*	1917	Hawthorn
Vampire (leader)	1917	White	*Vesper*	1918	Stephen
Vancouver	1918	Beardmore	*Vidette*	1918	Stephen
Vanessa	1918	Beardmore	*Vimiera*	1918	Swan Hunter
Vanity	1918	Beardmore	*Violent*	1918	Swan Hunter
Vanoc	1917	Clydebank	*Vittoria*	1918	Swan Hunter
Vanquisher	1917	Clydebank	*Vivacious*	1917	Yarrow
Vectis	1917	White	*Vivien*	1918	Yarrow
Vega	1917	Doxford	*Vortigern*	1918	White
Vehement	1917	Denny			
Velox	1917	Doxford			
Vendetta	1917	Fairfield			
Venetia	1917	Fairfield			

Below: HMS *Vivacious*, Admiralty 'V' class, leaving harbour 1920.
R. Perkins

Displacement: 1,090 tons
1,480 full load
Length: 312ft
Breadth: 29ft 6in
Draught: 10ft 10in
Armament: *Main* Four 4in (4×1) director controlled
AA One 3in, One MG
Tubes Four 21in (2×2)
Machinery: Geared turbines on two shafts giving
27,000shp
Max speed: 34kts
Fuel: 320-360 tons oil

Above: HMS *Vampire*, Admiralty 'V' class, at sea 1921. *R. Perkins*

Class Notes

This class was probably one of the most well known and successful to serve in the Royal Navy. The design was derived in part from the ex-Turkish ships. The 4in guns were mounted in the now well known A, B, X and Y positions and superimposed. The AA gun was aft of the second funnel. Some of this class were used as minelayers. HMS *Vampire* had six 21in tubes in two triple mountings.

Historical Notes

HMS *Valentine* was beached on the banks of the River Scheldt on 15 May 1940 after aircraft attack.

HMS *Vampire* (RAN) was sunk after surface action with vessels from a Japanese Task Force in the Bay of Bengal on 9 April 1942.

HMS *Vancouver* was renamed *Vimy* on being transferred to Canada in 1928.

HMS *Vehement* struck a mine and sank in the North Sea on 2 August 1918.

HMS *Venetia* struck a mine and sank in the Thames Estuary on 19 October 1940.

HMS *Verulam* struck a mine and sank off Seskaer Island in the Gulf of Finland on the night of 3/4 September 1919.

HMS *Vimiera* struck a mine and sank off the Nore on 9 January 1942.

HMS *Vittoria* was torpedoed by a Russian Bolshevik submarine in the Gulf of Finland on 1 September 1919.

HMS *Vortigern* was torpedoed by an E-boat off the east coast on 14 March 1942.

Admiralty 'W' Class

Unit	Completed	Builder	Unit	Completed	Builder
Voyager	1918	Stephen	*Westminster*	1918	Scotts
Wakeful	1917	Beardmore	*Whirlwind*	1918	Swan Hunter
Walker	1918	Denny	*Whitley*	1918	Doxford
Walpole	1918	Doxford	*Winchelsea*	1918	White
Walrus	1918	Fairfield	*Winchester*	1918	White
Warwick	1918	Hawthorn	*Windsor*	1918	Scotts
Watchman	1918	Beardmore	*Wolfhound*	1918	Fairfield
Waterhen	1918	Palmers	*Wrestler*	1918	Swan Hunter
Wessex	1918	Hawthorn	*Wryneck*	1918	Palmers
Westcott	1918	Denny			

Displacement: 1,100 tons
Length: 312ft
Breadth: 29ft 6in
Draught: 11ft
Armament: *Main* Four 4in, director controlled
Secondary One 3in
AA One MG
Tubes Six 21in (2×3)
Machinery: Geared turbines on two shafts giving 27,000shp
Max speed: 34kts
Fuel: 320-370 tons oil

Class Notes

This class was practically identical to the Admiralty 'V' class apart from having a taller mainmast and slightly greater displacement tonnage.

Historical Notes

HMS *Voyager* (RAN) was bombed by Japanese aircraft on 23 September 1942 and beached on Tumor Island.

Below: HMS *Wolfhound*, Admiralty 'W' class, at sea 1918.

Above: HMS *Watchman*, Admiralty 'W' class, 1920. Note minelaying stern. *R. Perkins*

HMS *Wakeful* sank off Nieuport after being hit by an E-boat torpedo on 29 May 1940.

HMS *Warwick* was torpedoed by a U-boat off Trevose Head on 20 February 1944.

HMS *Waterhen* whilst manned by the RAN, sank in tow on 30 June 1941 after aircraft attack in the eastern Mediterranean.

HMS *Wessex* sank after aircraft attack on 24 May 1940 near Calais.

HMS *Westcott* was the trials ship for the Hedgehog anti-submarine weapon in 1941.

HMS *Whirlwind* was torpedoed on 5 July 1940 by a U boat in thc western Mediterranean.

HMS *Whitley* was so named due to a typing error; her intended name was *Whitby*.

HMS *Whitley* was bombed and beached at Nieuport on 19 May 1940.

HMS *Wrestler* struck a mine and sank off the Normandy Beachhead on 6 June 1944.

HMS *Wryneck* sank after aircraft attack in the Gulf of Namplia on 27 April 1941.

Thornycroft 'V' and 'W' Class

Units: *Viceroy, Viscount, Wolsey, Woolston*
Completed: 1918
Builder: Thornycroft
Displacement: 1,120 tons
Length: 312ft
Breadth: 30ft 6in
Draught: 10ft 6in
Armament: *Main* Three 4in, director controlled
AA One 3in, One MG
Tubes Six 21in (2×3)
Machinery: Geared turbines on two shafts giving
30,000shp
Max speed: 35kts
Fuel: 320-370 tons oil

Class Notes
Although the four ships in this class had slightly more freeboard, and taller and broader after funnels, they were very similar to the 'V' and 'W' classes of Admiralty design. On deep load draught, their speed was the same, namely 31kts. This class had a shorter main mast than any other 'V' class destroyer.

HMS *Viceroy* and *Viscount* had four 21in tubes in twin mountings.

Below: HMS *Viscount*, Thornycroft 'V & W' class, at anchor 1920.
R. Perkins

Bottom: HMS *Wolsey*, Thornycroft 'V & W' class, at anchor 1920.
R. Perkins

Ex-Provisional Russian Government

Unit: *Derski*
Completed: 1913
Displacement: 1,100 tons
Length: 308ft
Breadth: 29ft 6in
Draught: 9ft
Armament: *Main* Three 4in (3×1)
AA One 9pdr
Tubes Ten 17.7in (5×2)
Machinery: Turbines on two shafts giving 25,500shp

Max speed: 34kts
Fuel: 255-280 tons oil

Class Notes
The *Derski* was quite a modern torpedo boat destroyer and is understood to have been built to a British design. She was taken over by the Royal Navy after the fall of Kerensky's Government until transfer was effected to the Naval force attached to General Denikin.

Thornycroft Modified 'W' Class

Units: *Wishart, Witch*
Commenced: 1918
Completed: *Wishart* 1920. *Witch* 1924
Builder: Thornycroft
Displacement: 1,140 tons
1,550 tons full load
Length: 312ft
Breadth: 30ft
Draught: 11ft
Armament: *Main* Four 4.7in, director controlled
AA One 3in, One MG
Tubes Six 21in (2 × 3)
Machinery: Geared turbines on two shafts giving 30,000shp

Max speed: 32kts
Fuel: 320-375 tons oil

Class Notes
With the exception of the staggered 2pdr mountings and the taller and broader fore funnel, there was very little difference between this class and the Thornycroft 'V' and 'W' class.

HMS *Wishart* had only three tubes.

HMS *Witch* although built and launched at Thornycrofts was fitted out and completed at HM Dockyard Devonport.

Above left: HMS *Wishart*, Thornycroft modified 'W' class, at anchor 1937. *R. Perkins*

Left: HMS *Witch*, Thornycroft modified 'W' class, entering harbour 1924.

Admiralty Modified 'W' Class

Unit	Completed	Builder
Vansittart	1920	Beardmore
Venomous (ex-*Venom*)	1919	Clydebank
Verity	1920	Clydebank
Veteran	1919	Clydebank
Vimy (ex-*Vantage*; later HMCS *Vancouver*)	1919	Beardmore
Volunteer	1919	Denny
Wanderer	1919	Fairfield
Whitehall	1920	Swan-Hunter*
Whitshed	1919	Swan-Hunter
Wild Swan	1919	Swan-Hunter
Witherington	1919	White
Wivern	1919	White
Wolverine	1920	White
Worcester	1922	White†
Wren	1919	Yarrow‡

* Completed by HM Dockyard, Chatham.
† Completed by HM Dockyard, Portsmouth.
‡ Completed by HM Dockyard, Pembroke.

Displacement: 1,120 tons
1,500 tons full load
Length: 312ft
Breadth: 29ft 6in
Draught: 11ft
Armament: *Main* Four 4.7in (4 × 1in shields)
AA Two 2pdr
Tubes Six 21in (2 × 3)
Machinery: Geared turbines on two shafts giving 27,000shp
Max speed: 34kts
Fuel: 320-375 tons oil

Below: HMS *Whitshed*, Admiralty modified 'W' class, leaving harbour 1919. *MoD (Navy)*

Bottom: HMS *Worcester*, Admiralty modified 'W' class, entering harbour. Photo shows *Worcester* as modified for escort duties during World War 2. *IWM*

Class Notes

Seven of this class had the same funnel arrangement as the 'V' class and seven as the 'W' class. The 2pdr guns were staggered aft of the second funnel. A very successful type with good service in World War 2.

All of this class had director control for the main armament. After the completion of this class in 1922, no other destroyers were launched until 1926.

Historical Notes

HMS *Wild Swan* sank on 17 June 1942 following an aircraft attack and later collision with a Spanish trawler — 100 miles west of the French coast.

HMS *Wren* sank after aircraft attack off the east coast of Aldeburgh on 27 July 1940.

HMS *Veteran* was torpedoed by a U-boat in the western Atlantic on 28 September 1942.

HMS *Worcester* struck a mine and was severely damaged on 23 December 1943 in the North Sea but made port and was used as the accommodation ship *Yeoman*.

Admiralty Large Design

Unit	Completed
Bruce	1918
Campbell	1918
Douglas	1918
Mackay	1919
Malcolm	1919
Montrose	1918
Scott	1917
Stuart	1918

Builder: Cammel-Laird (*Montrose* and *Stuart* Hawthorn-Leslie)
Displacement: 1,801 tons
Length: 322ft 6in
Breadth: 31ft 9in
Draught: 12ft 6in
Armament: *Main* Five 4.7in
Secondary One 3in AA
AA Two 2pdr, One MG
Tubes Six 21in (2 × 3)
Machinery: Geared turbines on two shafts giving 40,00shp
Max speed: 36.5kts
Fuel: 400-500 tons oil

Class Notes

In this class, both funnels were of the same height and were circular. *Barrington* and *Hughes,* both building at Cammell-Laird, were cancelled in 1918. Of a similar design to, but slightly larger than, the Thornycroft leaders ordered under the Emergency War Programme 1916-18, all of this class were built as leaders.

Historical Notes

HMS *Bruce* was expended as a target on 22 November 1939 off the Isle of Wight.

HMS *Scott* was torpedoed on 15 August 1918 by a U-boat in the North Sea off the Danish coast.

Below: HMS *Douglas*, Admiralty Large design, anchored 1924. *R. Perkins*

Above: HMS *MacKay*, Admiralty Large design, at sea 1919.   *R. Perkins*

Thornycroft Type

Unit	Completed
Broke (ex-*Rooke*)	1920
Keppel	1921
Shakespeare	1917
Spenser	1917
Wallace	1919

Builder: Thornycroft
Displacement: 1,480 tons
Length: 329ft
Breadth: 31ft 9in
Draught: 12ft 6in
Armament: *Main* Five 4.7in, director controlled
Secondary One 3in DP
AA Two 2pdr, One MG
Tubes Six 21in (2 × 3)
Machinery: geared turbines on two shafts giving 40,000shp
Max speed: 36kts
Fuel: 400-500 tons oil

Class Notes
This class, all of which were leaders, was similar in design to the Admiralty leaders of the previous class. *Saunders* and *Spragge* of this class, building at Thornycroft, were cancelled 1918. *Broke* was completed at HM Dockyard Pembroke and *Keppel* at Portsmouth.

Historical Notes
HMS *Broke* took part in a direct assault on Algiers Harbour during Operation 'Torch' on 8 November 1942, and in the best traditions cut through the boom and berthed safely alongside to land the troops she was carrying. Unfortunately, she sustained severe hits from the Vichy French batteries and sank the following day.

Below: HMS *Keppel*, Thornycroft Type, anchored 1929.   *R. Perkins*

Above: HMS *Broke*, Thornycroft Type, at sea 1920.

Thornycroft Experimental 'A' Class

Unit: *Amazon*
Commenced: 1925
Completed: 1926
Builders: Thornycroft
Displacement: 1,350 tons
Length: 311ft 9in PP
Breadth: 31ft 6in
Draught: 9ft 6in
Armament: *Main* Four 4.7in
Secondary Five .5in MG
AA One 3in
Tubes Six 21in (2 × 3)
Machinery: Geared turbines on two shafts giving 39,500shp

Max speed: 37kts
Fuel: 433 tons oil

Class Notes

HMS *Amazon* was Thornycrofts answer to the Admiralty's request for a destroyer design embodying all lessons learned during the war, and she was built under the 1924-25 estimate. She was fitted with Parsons low pressure turbines for cruising and was designed for home and tropical use with high freeboard and improved accommodation

Below: HMS *Amazon*, Thornycroft experimental 'A' class, at sea 1926.

Yarrow Experimental 'A' Class

Unit: *Ambuscade*
Commenced: 1924
Completed: 1926
Builders: Yarrow
Displacement: 1,170 tons
Length: 307ft PP
Breadth: 31ft
Draught: 8ft 3in
Armament: *Main* Four 4.7in
Secondary Five .5in MG
AA One 3in
Tubes Three 21in (1 × 3)
Machinery: Geared turbines on two shafts giving 33,000shp
Max speed: 35kts
Fuel: 385 tons oil

Class Notes

HMS *Ambuscade* was Yarrow's answer to the Admiralty's request for a destroyer design, embodying all lessons learned during the war, and was built under the 1924-25 estimate. She was fitted with Parsons low pressure turbines for cruising and was designed for home and tropical use with high freeboard and improved accommodation.

Below: HMS *Ambuscade*, Thronycroft experimental 'A' class, 1943. Note Squid in A position and radar above bridge. *MoD (Navy)*

'A' Class

Unit	Builder
Acasta	Clydebank
Achates	Clydebank
Acheron	Thornycroft
Active	Hawthorn-Leslie
Antelope	Hawthorn-Leslie
Anthony	Scotts SB
Ardent	Scotts SB
Arrow	Vickers Armstrong (Barrow)
Keith (leader)	Vickers Armstrong (Barrow)

Commenced: 1928 (*Keith* 1929)

Completed: 1930 (*Acheron* and *Keith* 1931)
Displacement: 1,375 tons (*Keith* 1,400)
Length: 323ft
Breadth: 32ft 9in (*Keith* 32ft 3in)
Draught: 8ft 6in
Armament: *Main* Four 4.7in
AA Two 2pdr, Five MG
Tubes Eight 21in (2×4)
Machinery: Geared turbines on two shafts giving 34,000shp
Max speed: 35.25kts (*Keith*)
Fuel: 380 tons oil (*Keith* 470)

Class Notes

This was the first full class to mount quadruple tubes. All ships easily passed their acceptance trials, and proved to be economical vessels. All of this class were fitted for high speed mine sweeping (HSMS).

Historical Notes

HMS *Acasta* took part in the action with the *Scharnhorst* and *Gneisenau*, and sank from shellfire on 8 June 1940.

HMS *Achates* foundered after heavy weather, following shellfire from the *Admiral Hipper* in the Barents Sea on 31 December 1942.

HMS *Acheron* sank after striking a mine in the English Channel, south of the Isle of Wight, on 8 December 1940.

HMS *Ardent* took part in the action with the *Scharnhorst* and *Gneisenau*, and sank from shellfire on 8 June 1940.

HMS *Arrow* was severely damaged when the SS *Port le Monte Algiers* exploded on 4 August 1943 and became a total loss.

HMS *Keith* sank after aircraft attack off Dunkirk on 1 June 1940.

Below: HMS *Arrow*, new 'A' class, at sea. *Vickers*

Bottom: HMS *Keith*, leader of the new 'A' class, at sea. *Vickers*

'B' Class

Units	Builder
Basilisk	Clydebank
Beagle	Clydebank
Blanche	Hawthorne-Leslie
Boadicea	Hawthorne-Leslie
Boreas	Palmers
Brazen	Palmers
Brilliant	Swan Hunter
Bulldog	Swan Hunter
Kempenfelt (leader)	White

Commenced: 1929 (*Kempenfelt* 1930)
Completed: 1931
Displacement: 1,360 tons (*Kempenfelt* 1,390)
Length: 323ft (*Kempenfelt* 326ft)
Breadth: 32ft 3in (*Kempenfelt* 33ft)
Draught: 8ft 6in (*Kempenfelt* 8ft 8in)
Armament: *Main* Four 4.7in
AA Two 2pdr, Five MG
Tubes Eight 21in (2×4)
Machinery: Geared turbines on two shafts giving 34,000shp (*Kempenfelt* 36,000shp)
Max speed: 34kts
Fuel: 380 tons oil (*Kempenfelt* 470)

Class Notes
All this class were very similar to the new 'A' class and were good economical ships.

Historical Notes
HMS *Basilisk* sank after aircraft attack off Dunkirk on 1 June 1940.

HMS *Blanche* was the first destroyer to be sunk in World War 2, this occurring on 13 November 1939 when she struck a mine in the Thames Estuary.

HMS *Boadicea* sank after aircraft attack off Portland on 13 June 1944.

HMS *Brazen* sank whilst in tow after aircraft attack off Dover on 20 July 1940.

Below: HMS *Boadicea*, new 'B' class, at anchor 1925. *R. Perkins*

Bottom: HMS *Bulldog*, new 'B' class, 1944. Note A and Y guns suppressed with radar, HF, MF, DF aerials on mainmast. *MoD (Navy)*

'C' Class

Units: *Comet, Crescent, Crusader, Cygnet*
Commenced: 1930
Completed: 1932
Builders: Vickers Armstrong (Barrow) (*Crescent, Cygnet*), HM Dockyard Portsmouth (*Crusader, Comet*)
Displacement: 1,375 tons
Length: 326ft
Breadth: 33ft
Draught: 8ft 6in
Armament: *Main* Four 4.7in
Secondary Seven smaller
Tubes Eight 21in (2×4)
Machinery: Geared turbines on two shafts giving 36,000shp
Max speed: 36kts
Fuel: 470 tons oil

Class Notes
General arrangement as the new 'D' class. These destroyers were transferred to the Royal Canadian Navy in 1937.

Historical Notes
HMCS *Fraser* (ex-*Crescent*) sank after collision with HMS *Calcutta* in the River Gironde on 28 June 1940.
HMCS *Ottawa* (ex-*Crusader*) was torpedoed by *U91* in the Gulf of St Lawrence on 14 September 1942.

Below: HMS *Crescent*, new 'C' class, at sea. Note HSMS gear on the stern. *Vickers*

Bottom: HMS *Crusader*, new 'C' class, at anchor 1927. Note detail of bridge director and searchlight on bandstand between the tubes; HSMS gear on the stern. *R. Perkins*

Admiralty Leader *Codrington*

Unit: *Codrington*
Commenced: 1928
Completed: 1930
Builder: Swan Hunter
Displacement: 1,540 tons
2,000 tons full load
Length: 332ft

Breadth: 33ft 9in
Draught: 12ft 3in
Armament: *Main* Five 4.7in
AA Two 2pdr, Five MGs
Tubes Eight 21in (2×4)
Machinery: Geared turbines on two shafts giving 39,000shp

Max speed: 35kts
Fuel: 500 tons oil

Class Notes

HMS *Codrington* attained the speed of 40kts on trials and in 1930, represented the ultimate in destroyer design; she was built under the 1927 programme.

Historical Notes

HMS *Codrington* was named to honour the centenary of the Battle of Navarino in 1827 at which Admiral Sir Edward Codrington was the Naval Commander in Chief.

HMS *Codrington* steamed from Scapa Flow to Dover, over 530 miles in under 24 hours, in 1940.

She saw service off the Netherlands and at Dunkirk and took on at least 2,000 men of the British Expeditionary Force. After the Norwegian Campaign the same year she was sunk by aircraft attack whilst in Dover Harbour on 27 July 1940.

'D' Class

Unit	Completed	Builder
Dainty	1933	Fairfield
Daring	1932	Thornycroft
Decoy	1933	Thornycroft
Defender	1932	Vickers Armstrong (Barrow)
Delight	1933	Fairfield
Diamond	1932	Vickers Armstrong (Barrow)
Diana	1932	Palmers
Duchess	1933	Palmers
Duncan (leader)	1933	HM Dockyard Portsmouth

Commenced: 1931
Displacement: 1,375 tons (*Duncan* 1,400)
Length: 326ft
Breadth: 33ft (*Duncan* 33ft 9in)
Draught: 8ft 6in
Armament: *Main* Four 4.7in

Below: HMS *Diamond*, 'D' class, at sea on builder's trials 1932. Note galley type funnels on port side of B gun blast shield and attached to the forward funnel. *Vickers*

Above: HMS *Defender*, 'D' class, on builder's trials off Walney Island. *Vickers*

Secondary Six smaller
Tubes Eight 21in (2 × 4)
Machinery: Geared turbines on two shafts giving 36,000shp (38,000shp in *Duncan*)
Max speed: 36kts (*Duncan* 36.75kts)
Fuel: 470 tons oil

Class Notes

HMS *Duncan* had crowsnests and a slightly different shaped bridge which included provision for a radar cabin.

Historical Notes

HMS *Dainty* sank after aircraft attack off Tobruk on 24 February 1941.

HMS *Daring* was torpedoed by a U-boat in the North Sea off Duncansby Head on 8 February 1940.

HMS *Decoy* later became HMCS *Kootenay*.

HMS *Defender* sank after air attack off Tobruk on 12 July 1941.

HMS *Delight* sank after aircraft attack off Dover on 29 July 1940.

HMS *Diamond* sank after aircraft attack in the Gulf of Nauplia on 27 April 1941.

HMS *Duchess* foundered after collision with HMS *Barham* off the West Scottish coast on 13 December 1939.

HMCS *Margaree* (ex-*Diana*) sank after collision with SS *Port Fairy* in the North Atlantic on 22 October 1940.

'E' Class

Unit	Builder
Echo	Denny
Eclipse	Denny
Electra	Hawthorn-Leslie
Encounter	Hawthorn-Leslie
Escapade	Scotts SB
Escort	Scotts SB
Esk	Swan-Hunter

Unit	Builder
Exmouth (leader)	HM Dockyard Portsmouth
Express	Swan Hunter

Commenced: 1933
Completed: 1934

Below: HMS *Encounter*, 'E' class, at anchor 1937. *R. Perkins*

Displacement: 1,350tons (*Escapade* 1,375 tons)
Length: 329ft (*Exmouth* 343ft)
Breadth: 33ft 3in (*Exmouth* 33ft 9in)
Draught: 8ft 6in (*Exmouth* 8ft 8in)
Armament: *Main* Four 4.7in
AA Six smaller
Tubes Eight 21in (2 × 4)
Machinery: Geared turbines on two shafts giving
36,000shp (*Exmouth* 38,000shp)
Max speed: 36kts (*Exmouth* 36.75kts)
Fuel: 490 tons oil (*Exmouth*)
Range: 6,000 miles at 15kts

Class Notes

Both of the leaders of this class and the 'F' class had a third 4.7in gun mounted on a deck house between the funnels, giving HMS *Exmouth* five 4.7in guns. HMS *Esk* and *Express* were equipped as minelayers and had a tripod main mast.

Above: HMS *Escapade*, 'E' class, 1945. Note A position Squid deleted by censor and Y gun suppressed. *MoD (Navy)*

Historical Notes

HMS *Echo* later became RHN *Navarinon*.

HMS *Eclipse* sank after striking a mine in the Aegean, east of Kalyminos, on 23 October 1943.

HMS *Electra* sank in action with Japanese surface vessels (including HIM *Jintsu*) in the Battle of the Java Sea on 27 February 1942.

HMS *Encounter* sank in action with Japanese cruisers HIM *Ashijara* and *Myoko* on 1 March 1942.

HMS *Escort* sank in tow after being torpedoed by a U-boat in the western Mediterranean on 11 July 1940.

HMS *Esk* sank after striking a mine in the North Sea on 1 September 1940.

HMS *Exmouth* sank after striking a mine in the Moray Firth on 21 January 1941.

HMS *Express* later became HMCS *Gatineau*.

'F' Class

Unit	Builder
Fame	Vickers Armstrong (Tyne)
Faulknor (leader)	Yarrow
Fearless	Cammell-Laird
Firedrake	Vickers Armstrong (Tyne)
Foresight	Cammell-Laird
Forester	White
Fortune	Clydebank
Foxhound	Clydebank
Fury	White

Commenced: 1933
Completed: 1935
Displacement: 1,360 tons (*Faulknor* 1,460 tons)
Length: 329ft 6in (*Faulknor* 340ft wl)
Breadth: 33ft 3in (*Faulknor* 33ft 9in)
Draught: 8ft 6in (*Faulknor* 8ft 6in)

Below: HMS *Fame*, 'F' class, entering harbour 1943. *MoD (Navy)*

Armament: *Main* Four 4.7in (*Faulknor* five)
AA Six smaller
Tubes Eight 21in (2 × 4)
Machinery: Geared turbines on two shafts giving 36,000shp (*Faulknor* 38,000shp)
Fuel: 490 tons oil
Range: 6,000 miles at 15kts (average)

Class Notes
This was virtually a repeat of the 1934 'E' class.

Historical Notes
HMS *Fearless* sank after being struck by an aircraft-launched torpedo whilst on convoy escort in the Mediterranean on 23 July 1941.

Above: HMS *Forester*, 'F' class, on Atlantic convoy duty 1942. *IWM*

HMS *Firedrake* was torpedoed by a U-boat in the western Atlantic on 17 December 1942.

HMS *Foresight* was struck by an aircraft-launched torpedo and not being salvable was despatched by own forces on 12 August 1942.

HMS *Fortune* later became HMCS *Saskatchewan*.

HMS *Foxhound* later became HMCS *Qu' Appelle*.

HMS *Fury* struck a mine and was damaged beyond repair off the Normandy beachhead on 21 June 1944.

'G' Class

Unit	Builder
Gallant	Stephen
Garland	Fairfield
Gipsy	Fairfield
Glowworm	Thornycroft
Grafton	Thornycroft
Grenade	Stephen
Grenville (leader)	Yarrow
Greyhound	Vickers Armstrong (Barrow)
Griffin	Vickers Armstrong (Barrow)

Commenced: 1934
Completed: 1936
Displacement: 1,335 tons (*Grenville* 1,485 tons)

Length: 323ft (*Grenville* 327ft wl)
Breadth: 34ft 6in
Draught: 8ft 3in (*Grenville* 8ft 8in)
Armament: *Main* Four 4.7in (*Grenville* Five)
AA Six smaller
Tubes Eight 21in (2 × 4)
Machinery: Geared turbines on two shafts giving 34,000shp (*Grenville* 38,000shp)
Max speed: 36kts (*Grenville* 36.5kts)
Fuel: 455 tons oil (*Grenville* 475)

Below: HMS *Glowworm*, 'G' class, at anchor 1937. *R. Perkins*

Above: HMS *Grafton*, 'G' class, at anchor 1937.   *R. Perkins*

Class Notes

All this class had tripod main masts and were very similar to the following 'H' class. HMS *Glowworm* was 1,345 tons displacement and had quintupled tubes (10.21in). She was the trials vessel for the quintuple torpedo tube mounting.

Historical Notes

HMS *Garland* was transferred to Poland in 1940.

HMS *Gallant* was hit by aircraft torpedoes on 10 June 1941 but proceeded to Grand Harbour, Malta. She sank after a further bombing attack on 20 June 1941.

HMS *Gipsy* struck a mine and sank off Harwich on 21 November 1939.

HMS *Glowworm*, after running short of ammunition, rammed and damaged the *Admiral Hipper* but was lost on 8 April 1940.

HMS *Grafton* was torpedoed by an E-boat and sank off Dunkirk on 29 May 1940.

HMS *Grenade* sank after aircraft attack off Dunkirk on 29 May 1940.

HMS *Grenville* struck a mine and sank in the North Sea on 20 January 1940.

HMS *Greyhound* sank after aircraft attack off Crete on 22 May 1941.

HMS *Griffin* later became HMCS *Ottawa*.

'H' Class

Unit	Builder
Hardy (leader)	Cammell-Laird
Hasty	Denny
Havock	Denny
Hereward	Vickers Armstrong (Tyne)
Hero	Vickers Armstrong (Tyne)
Hostile	Scotts SB
Hotspur	Scotts SB
Hunter	Swan Hunter
Hyperion	Swan Hunter

Commenced: 1935
Completed: 1936 (*Havock* 1937)
Displacement: 1,340 tons (*Hardy* 1,505 tons)
Length: 323ft (*Hardy* 334ft)
Breadth: 33ft (*Hardy* 34ft)
Draught: 8ft 6in (*Hardy* 8ft 8in)
Armament: *Main* Four 4.7in (*Hardy* Five)
AA Six smaller
Tubes Eight 21in (2 × 4)
Machinery: Geared turbines on two shafts giving 34,000shp (*Hardy* 38,000shp)

Max speed: 36kts (*Hardy* 36.75kts)
Fuel: 455 tons oil (*Hardy* 475)

Class Notes

Of very similar design to the 'G' class. HMS *Hero* had shorter funnels and a more streamlined bridge. HMS *Hereward* was the trials vessel for the twin 4.7in mounting for the 'Tribal' class.

Historical Notes

HMS *Hardy* (1936) foundered on 10 April 1940 after action with German destroyers Z2 and Z11 in the Battle of Narvik.

HMS *Hasty* sank on 15 June 1942 after aircraft attack whilst escorting a Mediterranean convey, being despatched by HMS *Hotspur*.

HMS *Havock* was wrecked on the Tunisian coast near Kelibia on 6 April 1942.

HMS *Hereward* sank on 29 May 1941 after aircraft attack off Crete.

HMS *Hero* later became HMCS *Chaudière*.

HMS *Hostile* struck a mine and sank off Malta on 23 August 1940.

HMS *Hunter* sank after action with German destroyers *Z2* and *Z11,* and collision with HMS *Hotspur* at Narvik, 10 April 1940.

HMS *Hyperion* struck a mine on 22 December 1940 off Pantellaria and was later sunk by HMS *Ilex*.

Top: HMS *Hurricane*, 'H' class, leaving Barrow after commissioning. The differences between the Brazilian (see p82) and British 'H' classes are apparent — altered bridge superstructure and armament. *Vickers*

Above: HMS *Hotspur*, 'H' class, at anchor 1943. *MoD (Navy)*

'I' Class

Unit	Builder	Unit	Builder
Icarus	Clydebank	*Inglefield* (leader)	Cammell-Laird
Ilex	Clydebank	*Intrepid*	White
Imogen	Hawthorn-Leslie	*Isis*	Yarrow
Imperial	Hawthorn-Leslie	*Ivanhoe*	Yarrow
Impulsive	White		

Commenced: 1936
Completed: 1937 (*Impulsive* 1938)
Displacement: 1,370 tons (*Inglefield* 1,530 tons)
Length: 320ft (*Inglefield* 334ft wl)
Breadth: 33ft (*Inglefield* 34ft)
Draught: 8ft 6in (*Inglefield* 8ft 8in)
Armament: *Main* Four 4.7in (*Inglefield* Five)
AA Six smaller
Tubes Ten 21in (2 × 5)
Machinery: Geared turbines on two shafts giving
34,000shp (*Inglefield* 38,000shp)
Max speed: 36kts (*Inglefield* 36.5kts)
Fuel: 455 tons oil (*Inglefield* 470)

Class Notes
All the ships in this class fitted for HSMS.

Historical Notes
HMS *Imogen* sank on 16 July 1940 after colliding in fog in
the Pentland Firth with HMS *Glasgow*.

HMS *Imperial* was attacked by enemy aircraft off Crete
on 29 May 1941. Disabled, she was later sunk by HMS
Hotspur.

HMS *Inglefield* was hit by a glider bomb launched by an
enemy aircraft and later sank off the Anzio beachhead on
25 February 1944.

HMS *Intrepid* sank after aircraft attack in the Aegean
on 26 September 1943.

HMS *Isis* struck a mine and sank off Normandy on
20 July 1944.

HMS *Ivanhoe* struck a mine on 1 September 1940 and
sank in the mouth of the River Texel.

Below: HMS *Imperial*, 'I' class, leaving harbour 1937. *R. Perkins*

Bottom: HMS *Intrepid*, 'I' class, without guns and flying builder's flag in
1937. *R. Perkins*

'Tribal' Class

Unit	Completed	Builder
Afridi (leader)	1938	Vickers Armstrong (Tyne)
Ashanti	1938	Denny
Bedouin	1939	Denny
Cossack (leader)	1938	Vickers Armstrong (Tyne)
Eskimo	1938	Vickers Armstrong (Tyne)
Gurkha	1938	Fairfield
Maori	1939	Fairfield
Mashona	1939	Vickers Armstrong (Tyne)
Matabele	1939	Scotts SB
Mohawk	1938	Thornycroft
Nubian	1938	Thornycroft
Punjabi	1939	Scotts SB
Sikh	1938	Stephen
Somali (leader)	1938	Swan Hunter
Tartar (leader)	1939	Swan Hunter
Zulu	1938	Stephen

Commenced: 1936 (*Bedouin* 1937)
Displacement: 1,870 tons
2,520 tons (full load)
Length: 355ft 6in
Breadth: 36ft 6in
Draught: 9ft
Armament: *Main* Eight 4.7in (4×2in shields)
AA Six smaller
Tubes Four 21in (1×4)

Below: HMS *Ashanti*, 'Tribal' class. Note twin 4.7in X mounting suppressed, and twin 4in DP/HA/AA mounting substituted. *IWM*

Bottom: HMS *Bedouin* 'Tribal' class, in Narvik Fjord 1940. Note X mounting twin 4.7in suppressed and twin 4in DP/HA/AA mounting substituted. *IWM*

Machinery: Geared turbines on two shafts giving 44,000shp
Max speed: 36.5kts
Fuel: 520 tons oil

Class Notes
The leaders were of similar appearance to the remainder. The 'Tribal' class of 1936 were the first Royal Naval destroyers to have their main armament in twin mountings. Both masts were tripod and these destroyers were the largest in tonnage since HMS *Codrington* of 1930. HMS *Larne* was renamed *Gurkha* in 1940, see 'Lightning' class.

Historical Notes
HMS *Afridi* sank on 3 May 1940 after aircraft attack off the coast of Norway.

HMS *Bedouin* was hit by an aircraft-launched torpedo on 15 June 1942 and later sunk by gunfire of own forces in the central Mediterranean.

HMS *Cossack* was torpedoed by a U-boat off Gibraltar on 27 October 1941.

HMS *Gurkha* was severely damaged by aircraft attack on 8 April 1940 and foundered off Bergen.

HMS *Maori* sank on 12 February 1942 after aircraft attack off Malta.

HMS *Mashona* sank on 28 May 1941 after aircraft attack off the west coast of Ireland.

HMS *Matabele* was torpedoed by a U-boat on 17 January 1942 off the North Cape.

HMS *Mohawk* was torpedoed by the Italian destroyer *Tarigo* on 16 April 1941 off Cape Bon.

HMS *Punjabi* sank after collision with HMS *King George V* in the Western Approaches on 8 May 1942.

HMS *Sikh* sank on 14 September 1942 after engaging enemy shore batteries at Tobruk.

HMS *Somali* sank in tow on 8 September 1942, three days after being torpedoed by enemy aircraft off the North Cape.

HMS *Zulu* whilst engaging shore batteries at Tobruk suffered severe damage and sank on 14 September 1942.

'Javelin' Class

J GROUP

Unit	Builder
Jackal	Clydebank
Jaguar	Denny
Janus	Swan Hunter
Javelin (ex-*Kashmir)*	Clydebank
Jersey	White
Jupiter	Yarrow
Juno (ex-*Jamaica*)	Fairfield
Jervis (leader)	Hawthorn-Leslie

Commenced: 1937
Completed: 1939
Displacement: 1,690 tons (*Jervis* 1,695 tons)
Length: 348ft
Breadth: 35ft

Below: HMS *Javelin*, 'Javelin' class J group, at anchor 1941. Note no radar and enveloping gunshields. *MoD (Navy)*

Above: HMS *Jervis*, 'Javelin' class J group, entering harbour 1945. *MoD (Navy)*

Draught: 9ft
Armament: *Main* Six 4.7in (3×2in shields)
AA Six smaller
Tubes Ten 21in (2×5)
Machinery: Geared turbines on two shafts giving 40,000shp
Max speed: 36kts
Fuel: 485 tons oil

Class Notes

The three groups of this class were based on the best points of the 'Intrepid' and 'Tribal' classes and were the first one funnel destroyer class since the 'A' class in 1895 which had *Zephyr* and *Fervent* with one funnel each. It was intended that this class would consist of eight private ships and one leader, but *Jubilant* was cancelled after the decision to build classes of eight was reached. She would have been built by White.

Historical Notes

HMS *Jackal* sank on 11 May 1942 after aircraft attack in the eastern Mediterranean.

HMS *Jaguar* was torpedoed by a U-boat off the coast of Libya on 26 March 1942.

HMS *Janus* whilst supporting the Pontine Landing sank after aircraft attack on 23 June 1944.

HMS *Jersey* struck a mine and sank in the entrance to Grand Harbour Malta on 2 May 1941.

HMS *Juno* sank on 20 May 1941 after aircraft attack off Crete.

HMS *Jupiter* attacked and sank the Japanese submarine *I60* on 17 January 1942 25 miles off Krakatoa, then on 27 February 1942 was torpedoed during the Battle of the Java Sea.

K GROUP

Unit	Builder
Kandahar	Denny
Kashmir (ex-Javelin)	Thornycroft
Kelly (leader)	Hawthorn-Leslie
Kelvin	Fairfield
Khartoum	Swan-Hunter
Kimberley	Thornycroft
Kingston	White
Kipling	Yarrow

Commenced: 1937 (*Kandahar* and *Kimberley* 1938)
Displacement: 1,690 tons
(*Kelly* 1,695 tons)
Length: 348ft
Breadth: 35ft
Draught: 9ft

Below: HMS *Kimberley*, 'Javelin' class K group, at sea. *MoD (Navy)*

Armament: *Main* Six 4.7in (2×3)
AA Six smaller
Tubes Ten 21in (2×5)
Machinery: Geared turbines on two shafts giving
40,000shp
Max speed: 36kts
Fuel: 485 tons oil

Class Notes
All built to the same design as the 'J' group.

Historical Notes
HMS *Khandahar* struck a mine on 19 December 1941
off the coast of Libya and sank on 20 December 1941.

Above: HMS *Kelly*, 'Javelin' class K group, on trials. *Swan Hunter*

HMS *Kashmir* sank after aircraft attack off Crete on
22 May 1941.
HMS *Kelly* sank after aircraft attack off Crete on
23 May 1941.
HMS *Khartoum* on 23 June 1940 was on patrol off
Perim when the air vessel of the starboard torpedo
mounting exploded causing an uncontrollable fire,
necessitating beaching the ship and abandonment.
HMS *Kingston* was hit on 11 April 1942 in a bombing
raid on Valetta Harbour and destroyed.
HMS *Kipling* sank after aircraft attack in the eastern
Mediterranean on 11 May 1942.

N GROUP

Unit	Builder
Napier (leader)	Fairfield
Nerissa	John Brown
Nestor	Fairfield
Nizam	John Brown
Noble (ex-*Nerissa*)	John Brown
Nonpareil	Denny
Norman	Thornycroft
Norseman	Thornycroft

Commenced: 1939
Completed: 1941 (*Nerissa* and *Napier* 1940)
Displacement: 1,690 tons (*Napier* 1,695 tons)
Length: 348ft
Breadth: 35ft
Draught: 9ft
Armament: *Main* Six 4.7in in shields
AA Four 40mm
Six 20mm

Tubes Ten 21in (2 × 5)
AS 30 DCs carried
Machinery: Geared turbines on two shafts giving
40,000shp
Max speed: 36kts
Fuel: 500 tons oil

Class Notes
HMS *Noble* and *Nonpareil* were the second of the name in
this class, the earlier constructions having been sold to the
Netherlands. A number of this class were completed with
a 4in gun in place of the after tubes. All ships had
improved AA firepower.

Historical Notes
HMS *Nerissa* was transferred to Poland as *Piorun*.
HMS *Nestor* (whilst under RAN) sank after aircraft
attack on 15 June 1942 escorting a Malta convoy.
HMS *Norseman* was renamed *Nepal* in recognition of
services by that Kingdom to the war effort.

Top: HMS *Nizam*, 'Javelin' class N group, at sea. *MoD (Navy)*

Above: HMS *Norman*, 'Javelin' class N group, at sea. Note main batteries and pennant number deleted by censor. *MoD (Navy)*

'Lightning' Class

L GROUP

Unit	Builder
Laforey (leader)	Yarrow
Lance	Yarrow
Larne (later *Gurkha (2)*)	Cammell-Laird
Legion	Hawthorn-Leslie
Lightning	Hawthorn-Leslie
Lively	Cammell-Laird
Lookout	Scotts SB
Loyal	Scotts SB

Commenced: 1938
Completed: 1940 (*Larne* and *Laforey* 1941)
Displacement: 1,920 tons (*Laforey* 1,935 tons)
Length: 354ft
Breadth: 37ft
Draught: 10ft

Armament: *Main* Six 4.7in (3 × 2 in turrets at A, B, X positions *Lightning, Lookout, Loyal*)
Eight 4in (2 × 4 in shields at A, B, X, Y positions *Lance, Larne, Legion, Lively*)
Secondary Six smaller
Tubes Eight 21in (2 × 4)
AS Two DC racks on stern, four throwers port and starboard at X, Y positions.
30 DCs carried
Machinery: Geared turbines on two shafts giving 45,000shp
Max speed: 36.5kts

Class Notes
The Y 4in guns were on the same deckhouse as those in the X position. The 4.7in had 45° elevation, the 4in being

AA weapons with 80° elevations. The 4.7in guns could be elevated and depressed independently.

HMS *Laforey* was armed with twin 4.7in guns (3×2) in turrets at A, B and X positions, with a single 4in HA/QF mounted in lieu of the after torpedo tubes.

Top: HMS *Lookout*, 'Lightning' class L group, at anchor 1942. *MoD (Navy)*

Above: HMS *Loyal*, 'Lightning' class L group, at anchor with no radar 1942. *MoD (Navy)*

Historical Notes

HMS *Laforey* was torpedoed on 30 March 1944 by a U-boat off the north coast of Sicily and later sunk.

HMS *Lance* was badly damaged on 22 October 1942 during an air attack on Malta, but was towed to the UK and broken up in 1944.

HMS *Larne* was later renamed *Gurkha (2)* and as this was torpedoed by a U-boat on 17 January 1942 off Libya.

HMS *Legion* sank on 25 March 1942 after aircraft attack at Malta.

HMS *Lightning* was torpedoed on 12 March 1943 by an Italian MTB off the Libyan Coast.

HMS *Lively* sank after aircraft attack on 11 May 1942 in the eastern Mediterranean.

HMS *Loyal* struck a mine off the north-east coast of Italy on 12 October 1944, became a constructive total loss and in 1948 was towed to the UK for breaking.

M GROUP

Unit	Builder	Unit	Builder
Marksman (later *Mahratta*)	Scotts SB	*Milne* (leader)	Scotts SB (completed by John Brown & Co)
Marne	Vickers Armstrong (Tyne)		
Martin	Vickers Armstrong (Tyne)	*Musketeer*	Fairfield
Matchless	Stephen	*Myrmidon*	Fairfield
Meteor	Stephen		

Commenced: 1940 (*Marne* 1939)
Completed: 1941 (*Marne* and *Martin* 1940)
Displacement: 1,920 tons (*Milne* 1,935 tons)
Length: 362ft 6in
Breadth: 37ft
Draught: 10ft
Armament: *Main* Six 4.7in (3 × 2 in turrets)
AA One 4in
Four 2pdr
Ten 20mm
Tubes Four 21in (1 × 4)
Machinery: Geared turbines on two shafts giving
48,000shp
Max speed: 36kts

Class Notes

HMS *Marne* and *Matchless* did not carry the 4in gun and
did carry eight 21in quadrupled tubes.

This group was the first to mount the main armament
in turrets and the guns were power operated.

Historical Notes

The Mahratta Brigade of the Indian Army requested that
a ship of the Fleet should bear their name, and to comply,
and in tribute, the *Marksman* was renamed *Mahratta*.

HMS *Mahratta* (ex-*Marksman*) was torpedoed by a
U-boat on 25 February 1944 when escorting a North
Russian convoy.

HMS *Martin* was torpedoed by a U-boat at the Algerian
Landings on 10 November 1942.

HMS *Myrmidon* served with the Polish Navy and was
renamed *Orkan*, but was torpedoed on 5 October 1943 in
the North Atlantic.

Below: HMS *Marne*, 'Lightning' class M group, leaving harbour 1942.
MoD (Navy)

Bottom: HMS *Musketeer*, 'Lightning' class M group, at sea on convoy
duty 1942. *MoD (Navy)*

'Towns' Class

CRAVEN TYPE

Unit	Builder
Lewes (ex-USS *Conway*, ex-USS *Craven*)	Bethlehem SB
St Marys (ex-USS *Bagley*)	Norfolk NY

Commenced: 1918
Completed: 1919
Displacement: 1,020 tons
Length: 342ft
Breadth: 35ft

Draught: 9ft
Armament: *Main* Four 5in (51cal)
Secondary Two 3in (23cal)
AA Four MGs
Tubes 12 21in (4×3)
Machinery: Geared turbines on two shafts giving 25,000shp
Max speed: 35kts
Fuel: 400 tons oil

TYPE 4

Unit	Commenced	Completed	Builder	Unit	Commenced	Completed	Builder
Belmont (ex-USS *Saterlee*)	1918	1919	Newport News SB	*Clare* (ex-USS *A. P. Upshur*)	1918	1920	Newport News SB
Beverley (ex-USS *Branch*)	1918	1920	Newport News SB	*Ramsey* (ex-USS *Meade*)	1918	1919	Bethlehem SB
Bradford (ex-USS *McLanahan*)	1918	1919	Bethlehem SB	*Reading* (ex-USS *Bailey*)	1918	1919	Bethlehem SB
Broadwater (ex-USS *Mason*)	1918	1920	Newport News SB	*Ripley* (ex-USS *Shubrick*)	1918	1919	Bethlehem SB
Broadway (ex-USS *Hunt*)	1918	1920	Newport News SB	*Rockingham* (ex-USS *Swasey*)	1918	1919	Bethlehem SB
Burnham (ex-USS *Aulick*)	1918	1919	Bethlehem SB	*St Croix* (ex-USS *McCook*)	1918	1919	Bethlehem SB
Burwell (ex-USS *Lamb*)	1918	1919	Bethlehem SB	*St Francis* (ex-USS *Bancroft*)	1918	1919	Bethlehem SB
Buxton (ex-USS *Edwards*)	1918	1919	Bethlehem SB	*Sherwood* (ex-USS *Rodgers*)	1918	1919	Bethlehem SB
Cameron (ex-USS *Welles*)	1918	1919	Bethlehem SB	*Stanley* (ex-USS *McCalla*)	1918	1919	Bethlehem SB
Chesterfield (ex-USS *W. C. Wood*)	1918	1920	Newport News SB				
Churchill (ex-USS *Herndon*)	1918	1920	Newport News SB				

Below: HMS *Ramsey* (ex-American) 'Towns' class, leaving for the Atlantic 1942. *MoD (Navy)*

TYPE 5

Unit	Com-menced	Com-pleted	Builder	Unit	Com-menced	Com-pleted	Builder
Caldwell (ex-USS *Hale*)	1918	1919	Bath Iron Works	*Lincoln* (ex-USS *Yarnall*)	1918	1918	Wm Cramp & Sons
Campbeltown (ex-USS *Buchanan*)	1918	1919	Bath Iron Works	*Mansfield* (ex-USS *Evans*)	1917	1918	Bath Iron Works
Castleton (ex-USS *Aaron Ward*)	1918	1919	Bath Iron Works	*Montgomery* (ex-USS *Wickes*)	1917	1918	Bath Iron Works
Chelsea (ex-USS *Crowninshield*)	1918	1919	Bath Iron Works	*Richmond* (ex-USS *Fairfax*)	1917	1918	Mare Is Navy Yd
Lancaster (ex-USS *Philip*)	1917	1918	Bath Iron Works	*Salisbury* (ex-USS *Claxton*)	1918	1919	Mare Is Navy Yd
Leamington (ex-USS *Twiggs*)	1918	1919	New York SB	*Wells* (ex-USS *Tillman*)	1918	1921	Charleston N Yd

TYPE 6

Unit	Com-menced	Com-pleted	Builder	Unit	Com-menced	Com-pleted	Builder
Annapolis (ex-USS *Mackenzie*)	1918	1919	Union Iron Works	*Newark* (ex-USS *Ringgold*)	1918	1919	Union Iron Works
Bath (ex-USS *Hopewell*)	1918	1919	Newport News SB	*Newmarket* (ex-USS *Robinson*)	1917	1918	Union Iron Works
Brighton (ex-USS *Cowell*)	1918	1919	Bethlehem SB	*Newport* (ex-USS *Sigourney*)	1917	1918	Bethlehem SB
Charlestown (ex-USS *Haraden*)	1918	1919	Newport News SB	*Niagara* (ex-USS *Thatcher*)	1918	1919	Bethlehem SB
Columbia (ex-USS *Haraden*)	1918	1919	Seattle Dry Dock	*Roxborough* (ex-USS *Foote*)	1918	1919	Bethlehem SB
Georgetown (ex-USS *Maddox*)	1918	1919	Bethlehem SB	*St Albans* (ex-USS *Thomas*)	1918	1919	Newport News SB
Hamilton (ex-USS *Kalk*)	1918	1919	Bethlehem SB	*St Clair* (ex-USS *Williams*)	1918	1919	Union Iron Works

TYPE 7

Unit	Com-menced	Com-pleted	Builder	Unit	Com-menced	Com-pleted	Builder
Leeds (ex-USS *Conner*)	1916	1918	Wm Cramp & Sons	*Ludlow* (ex-USS *Stockton*)	1916	1918	Wm Cramp & Sons

TYPES 4, 5, 6 and 7

Displacement: 1,190 tons (Type 4)
1,090 tons (Type 5)
1,060 tons (Type 6)
1,020 tons (Type 7)
Length: 314ft 6in
315ft 6in (Type 7)
Breadth: 30ft 6in
Draught: 9ft 9in (Type 4)
8ft 9in (Type 5)
8ft 6in (Type 6)
7ft 6in (Type 7)
Armament: *Main* Four 4in (50cal)

Five 4in (Type 7; two paired on forecastle)
Secondary One 3in (23cal)
Tubes 12 21in (3×4)
Machinery: Geared turbines on two shafts giving
27,000shp (20,000shp Type 7)
Max speed: 35kts
30kts (Type 7)
Fuel: 375 tons oil
260 tons oil (Type 7)

Class Notes
These destroyers were transferred to the RN under the

Above: HMS *Leeds*, (ex-American) 'Towns' class; note A gun zareba, 1942. *MoD (Navy)*

terms of the agreement of 2 September 1940, between the Governments of the UK and the USA. On transfer, with the exception of HMS *Ludlow* which had three funnels, and HMS *Bradford* which had two funnels, all had four. These destroyers were named after towns and villages with common names in both countries.

Historical Notes
The following vessels were transferred to the USSR in 1942: HMS *Chelsea* transferred as *Derzki*, *Roxborough* as *Dublestini*, *St Albans* as *Doistoini*, *Brighton* as *Zharki*, *Leamington* as *Zhguchi*, *Richmond* as *Zhivuchi*, *Georgetown* as *Zhostki*, and *Lincoln* for spares.

HMS *Bath* was torpedoed by a U-boat whilst escorting a north Russian convoy on 19 August 1941.

HMS *Belmont* was torpedoed by a U-boat in the North-Western Approaches on 31 December 1941.

HMS *Beverley* was torpedoed by a U-boat south of Greenland on 10 April 1943 having collided the previous day with the SS *Cairnrona*.

HMS *Broadwater* was torpedoed by a U-boat in the western Atlantic on 18 October 1941.

HMS *Cameron* sank after aircraft attack at Portsmouth on 15 December 1940.

HMS *Campbeltown* won immortality by ramming and blowing the outer gates of the Normandie Lock at St Nazaire on 28 March 1942.

Deiatelnyi (ex-HMS *Churchill*) whilst on loan to the USSR was torpedoed in the Arctic on 16 January 1945.

HMS *Rockingham* on 27 September 1944 struck a mine and sank off Aberdeen.

HMS *Sherwood* was expended as an air target in May 1943.

HMS *Stanley* was torpedoed by a U-boat in the Atlantic on 18 December 1941.

HMS *St Croix* (later HMCS) was torpedoed by *U305* south of Iceland on 20 September 1943.

HMS *St Francis* (later HMCS) sank after collision with the SS *Winding Gulf* off Sagonnet point on 14 July 1943.

Ex-French

Unit: *Leopard* (ex-*Léopard*)
Commenced: 1922
Completed: 1927
Builders: Ch de Loire, St Nazaire
Displacement: 2,126 tons
2,700 tons (full load)
Length: 416ft
Breadth: 37ft 6in
Draught: 17ft 6in
Armament: *Main* Five 5.1in
AA Eight 13mm
Tubes Six 21.7in (2×3)
Machinery: Turbines on two shafts giving 55,000shp
Max speed: 35.5kts
Range: 900 miles at full speed
Fuel: 550 tons oil

Class Notes
This ship served under the White Ensign in 1940 but was

returned to the Free French Navy later on. A typical French design, with three black cowled raked funnels. She had a greater length than any contemporary RN destroyer.

By the Washington Treaty, this ship would have rated as a cruiser being above 2,000 tons standard displacement tonnage.

Historical Notes
HMS *Leopard* served between May and July 1940 with the Portsmouth local flotilla and was manned from HMS *Victory*.

FFS *Léopard* was wrecked near Tobruk on 27 May 1943.

Eight other French destroyers served under the White Ensign from two classes — the 'Pomone' and 'Simoun' Classes. All (except *Brandelbras* which was lost) were returned to the French after the war.

Above: HMS *Leopard* (ex-French) at Belfast Lough. *IWM*

'POMONE' CLASS

Unit	Builder
H *Brandelbras*	Normand
H20 *Bouclier*	Ch Worms
H25 *La Cordelière*	Normand
H63 *La Flore*	At & Ch Bretagne
H47 *L'Incomprise*	Ch Worms
H56 *La Melpomone*	At & Ch Bretagne

Completed: 1935-36
Displacement: 610 tons
Length: 294ft 3in
Breadth: 23ft 9in
Draught: 9ft 3in
Armament: *Main* Two 3.9in (2×1)

Secondary Two 37mm (2×1)
AA Four 13mm (2×2)
Tubes Two 21.7in (1×2)
Machinery: Geared turbines on two shafts giving 22,000shp
Max speed: 34kts

Historical Notes
Brandelbras used as a harbour training ship at Portsmouth as were all the others except *La Melpomone* which was at the Nore.

Brandelbras foundered in bad weather in the English Channel, 14 December 1940.

'SIMOUN' CLASS

Unit	Builder
H03 *Mistral*	F & Ch de la Med (Havre)
H16 *Ouragan*	Ch Navales Français

Completed: 1924-26
Displacement: 1,319 tons
Length: 325ft 3in
Breadth: 33ft 3in
Draught: 13ft 9in
Armament: *Main* Four 5.1in (4×1)
AA Two 37mm (2×1)

Tubes Six 21.7in (2×3)
Machinery: Geared turbines on two shafts giving 33,000shp
Max speed: 33kts

Historical Notes
Mistral was used as tender to HMS *Cardiff* for gunnery training.

Ouragan was used as harbour training ship at Portsmouth.

Ex-Dutch

Unit	Completed	Builder
H35 (ex-*G13*)	1913	De Schelde
H66 (ex-*G15*)	1914	Fijenoord

Displacement: 150 tons
Length: 162ft 6in
Breadth: 17ft

Draught: 4ft 6in
Armament: *Main* Two 3in (2×1)
Tubes Three 17.7in (3×1)
Machinery: Reciprocating VTE on one shaft giving 5,500ihp
Max speed: 25kts

Historical Notes
H35 was used as a harbour service craft with the 2nd Submarine Flotilla.
H66 was used as a harbour service craft.

Units: H97 *Blade* (ex-*Z5*), H- (ex-*Z6*), H93 (ex-*Z7*), H71 (ex-*Z8*)
Completed: 1915
Builder: De Schelde
Displacement: 264 tons
Length: 192ft
Breadth: 19ft 9in
Draught: 5ft 6in
Armament: *Main* Two 3in (2×1)
AA Two MGs (2×1)
Tubes Four 17.7in (1×2, 2×1)
H97 had no tubes
Machinery: Reciprocating VTE on two shafts giving 5,500ihp (H97 3,000ihp)

Max speed: 27kts
22kts (H97)

Historical Notes
RN service covered Plymouth 8th and Harwich 16th Flotillas and the Reserve Fleet, Home Ports.
H97 *Blade* was used as a tender for the 7th Submarine Flotilla.
H- was used as a harbour service craft at Rosyth and Greenock.
H93 was used as a harbour service craft at Rosyth.
H71 was used as a tender to the 1st and later the 7th Submarine Flotilla.

'Hunt' Class

The 'Hunt' class comprised Types 1-4, all designed as convoy escorts, with anti-aircraft capabilities. Nevertheless, they did have an anti-submarine role, destroying five Italian submarines (*Amiraglio Caracciolo, Asteria, Galileo Ferrari, Maggiori Baracca, Narvalo*) and 16 German ones (*U131, U223, U371, U372, U413, U434, U443, U450, U453, U458, U559, U562, U568, U587, U593, U671*) — this despite the lack of a 'Hedgehog'. A 2pdr manual bow-chaser was fitted for service on East Coast escorts. Of the 'Hunt' class, 86 were completed, 14 transferred to other Allied Navies (see below) and 72 commissioned by the RN.

Destroyers of the 'Hunt' class transferred to other Allied navies were: *Bolebrook* to Greece as *Pindou*; *Border* to Greece as *Adrias*; *Bedale* to Poland as *Slazak*; *Catterick* to Greece as *Hastings*; *Hatherleigh* to Greece as *Canaris*; *Modbury* to Greece as *Miaoulis*; *Glaisdale* to Norway as *Glaisdale*; *Eskdale* to Norway as *Eskdale*; *Haldon* to France as *La Combattante*; *Oakley (1)* to Poland as *Kujawiak*; *Silverton* to Poland as *Krakowiak*; *Badsworth* to Norway as *Arendal*; *Bramham* to Greece as *Themistocles*; *Hursley* to Greece as *Kriti*.

Right: HMS *Atherstone*, 'Hunt' class Type 1, at launch.
Cammell-Laird SB

TYPE 1

Unit	Completed	Builder
Atherstone	1940	Cammell-Laird
Berkeley	1940	Cammell-Laird
Cattistock	1940	Yarrow
Cleveland	1941	Yarrow
Cotswold	1941	Yarrow
Cottesmore	1940	Yarrow
Eglinton	1940	Vickers-Armstrong (Tyne)
Exmoor	1940	Vickers-Armstrong (Tyne)
Fernie	1941	John Brown
Garth	1940	John Brown
Hambledon	1940	Swan Hunter
Holderness	1940	Swan Hunter
Mendip	1940	Swan Hunter
Meynell	1940	Swan Hunter
Pytchley	1940	Scotts SB
Quantock	1940	Scotts SB
Quorn	1940	White
Southdown	1940	White
Tynedale	1940	Stephen
Whaddon	1941	Stephen

Commenced: 1939
Displacement: 1,000 tons
Length: 280ft
Breadth: 29ft
Draught: 7ft 9in
Armament: *Main* Four 4in
Secondary Four 2pdr
AA Two 20mm
AS 70 DCs carried

Machinery: Geared turbines on two shafts giving 19,000shp
Max speed: 30kts
Range: 2,000 miles at 12kts
Fuel: 280 tons oil

Class Notes

This class of destroyer was designed as a convoy escort but was unable to cross the Atlantic without RAS which was in its infancy in the early years of World War 2. The 'Hunt' class saw the end, for the time being of the trend towards large tonnage destroyers.

Historical Notes

HMS *Berkeley* was severely damaged off Dieppe by aircraft attack, and had to be sunk by own forces.

HMS *Exmoor* was torpedoed by an E-boat off Lowestoft and sank on 25 February 1941.

HMS *Quorn* sank after the warhead from a German human torpedo was attached and detonated, whilst she was on patrol off the Normandy Beachhead on 2 August 1944.

HMS *Tynedale* was torpedoed by a U-boat on 12 December 1943 in the Western Mediterranean.

Below: HMS *Eglington*, 'Hunt' class Type 1, at sea; note bowchaser. *MoD (Navy)*

TYPE 2

Unit	Commenced	Completed	Builder	Unit	Commenced	Completed	Builder
Avonvale	1940	1941	John Brown	*Blencathra*	1939	1940	Cammell Laird
Badsworth	1940	1941	Cammell Laird	*Bramham*	1941	1942	Stephen
Beaufort	1939	1941	Cammell Laird	*Brocklesby*	1939	1941	Cammell Laird
Bedale	1940	1942	Hawthorn Leslie	*Calpe*	1941	1942	Swan Hunter
Bicester	1940	1941	Hawthorn Leslie	*Chiddingfold*	1940	1941	Scotts SB
Blackmore	1941	1942	Stephen	*Cowdray*	1940	1942	Scotts SB
Blankney	1941	1942	John Brown	*Croome*	1940	1941	Stephen

Unit	Commenced	Completed	Builder
Dulverton	1940	1941	Stephen
Eridge	1939	1940	Swan Hunter
Exmoor (2) (ex-*Burton*)	1940	1941	Swan Hunter
Farndale	1939	1941	Swan Hunter
Grove	1939	1941	Swan Hunter
Heythrop	1939	1941	Swan Hunter
Hursley	1940	1941	Swan Hunter
Hurworth	1939	1941	Vickers Armstrong (Tyne)
Lamerton	1939	1940	Swan Hunter
Lauderdale	1940	1941	Thornycroft
Ledbury	1940	1942	Thornycroft
Liddesdale	1939	1940	Vickers Armstrong (Tyne)
Middleton	1940	1941	Vickers Armstrong (Tyne)
Oakley (1)	1940	1941	Vickers Armstrong (Tyne)
Puckeridge	1940	1941	White
Silverton	1939	1941	White
Southwold	1940	1942	White
Tetcott	1940	1941	White
Tickham	1941	1942	Yarrow
Wheatland	1940	1941	Yarrow
Wilton	1941	1942	Yarrow
Zetland	1941	1942	Yarrow

Displacement: 1,025 tons
1,490 tons (full load)
Length: 280ft
Breadth: 31ft 6in
Draught: 7ft 6in

Armament: *Main* Six 4in (3×2)
AA Two 40mm (2×1), Four 2pdr (1×4)
AS Four DC throwers 60 DCs carried
Machinery: Geared turbines on shafts giving 19,000shp
Max speed: 29kts
Range: 3,600nm radius or 14kts
Fuel: 275 tons oil

Class Notes
This was the second class of utility escort destroyer for rapid construction. The Type 2s escorted Atlantic convoys.

Historical Notes
HMS *Dulverton* sank after being hit by a glider bomb off Kos on 13 November 1943.

HMS *Grove* sank on 15 June 1942 after aircraft attack in the central Mediterranean.

HMS *Heythrop* was torpedoed by a U-boat off the Libyan Coast on 20 March 1942.

HMS *Hurworth* struck a mine and sank in the Aegean on 22 October 1943.

HMS *Oakley (1)* became HMS *Kujawiak* and as such was sunk in the central Mediterranean on 15 June 1942 after aircraft attack.

HMS *Puckeridge* was torpedoed by a U-boat in the western Mediterranean on 6 September 1943.

HMS *Southwold* struck a mine on 24 March 1942 and sank off Malta.

HMS *Tickham* later became HMS *Oakley (2)*.

Below: HMS *Badsworth* 'Hunt' class Type 2, leaving the fitting out basin under tow on the River Mersey. *Cammell-Laird SB*

Top: HMS *Bedale*, 'Hunt' class Type 2, entering harbour 1943.
MoD (Navy)

Above: HMS *Zetland* 'Hunt' class Type 2 1943; note AA radar.
MoD (Navy)

TYPE 3

Unit	Com-menced	Com-pleted	Builder	Unit	Com-menced	Com-pleted	Builder
Airedale	1941	1942	John Brown	*La Combattante*	1941	1942	Fairfield
Albrighton	1940	1941	John Brown	(ex-*Haldon*)			
Aldenham	1941	1942	Cammell-Laird	*Hatherleigh*	1940	1941	Vickers
Belvoir	1940	1942	Cammell-Laird				Armstrong (Tyne)
Blean	1941	1942	Hawthorn-Leslie	*Haydon*	1941	1942	Vickers
Bleasdale	1940	1941	Vickers				Armstrong (Tyne)
			Armstrong (Tyne)	*Holcombe*	1941	1942	Stephen
Bolebrook	1940	1941	Swan Hunter	*Limbourne*	1941	1942	Stephen
Border	1941	1942	Swan Hunter	*Melbreak*	1941	1942	Swan Hunter
Catterick	1940	1941	Vickers	*Modbury*	1941	1942	Swan Hunter
			Armstrong (Barrow)	*Penylan*	1941	1942	Vickers
Derwent	1940	1941	Vickers				Armstrong (Barrow)
			Armstrong (Barrow)	*Rockwood*	1941	1942	Vickers
Easton	1941	1942	White				Armstrong (Barrow)
Eggesford	1941	1942	White	*Stevenstone*	1941	1943	White
Eskdale	1941	1942	Cammell-Laird	*Talybont*	1941	1943	White
Glaisdale	1941	1942	Cammell-Laird	*Tanatside*	1941	1942	Yarrow
Goathland	1942	1943	Fairfield	*Wensleydale*	1941	1942	Yarrow

Top: HMS *Aldenham*, 'Hunt' class Type 3, leaving the fitting out basin on the River Mersey. *Cammell-Laird SB*

Above: HMS *Catterick*, 'Hunt' class Type 3, leaving harbour passing Walney Island. Aft of the funnel may be seen the multiple pompom on its own deckhouse. *Vickers*

Below: HMS *Derwent*, 'Hunt' class Type 3, leaving harbour passing Walney Island. The RDF antenna is positioned below and forward of the bridge, the supporting structure being between the magazine ventilator cowls. *Vickers*

Displacement: 1,037 tons
Length: 280ft
Breadth: 31ft 3in
Draught: 7ft 3in
Armament: *Main* Four 4in (2×2)
AA Four 2pdr, Two 20mm (or 40mm)
Tubes Two 21in
AS Four DC throwers
60 DCs carried
Machinery: Geared turbines on twin shafts giving 19,000shp
Max speed: 28kts
Range: 3,700 miles radius at 14kts
Fuel: 275 tons oil

Historical Notes

HMS *Airedale* was torpedoed by a U-boat in the central Mediterranean on 16 June 1942.

HMS *Aldenham* struck a mine on 14 December and sank in the Adriatic.

HMS *Blean* was torpedoed by a U-boat off Oran on 11 December 1942.

HMS *Eskdale* whilst in Norwegian service was torpedoed on 14 April 1943 by an E-boat off the Lizard, in the English Channel.

HMS *Haldon* (*La Combattante*) struck a mine in the North Sea on 23 February 1945.

HMS *Holcombe* was torpedoed by *U593* off Bougie on 12 December 1943.

HMS *Limbourne* was torpedoed on 23 October 1943 by an E-boat in the English Channel and later sunk by own forces.

HMS *Penylan* was torpedoed by an E-boat in the English Channel on 2 December 1942.

TYPE 4

Units: *Brecon, Brissenden*
Commenced: 1941
Completed: 1942
Builder: Thornycroft
Displacement: 1,175 tons
Length: 296ft
Breadth: 33ft 6in
Draught: 9ft
Armament: *Main* Six 4in (3×2)
AA Four 2pdr
Two 40mm
Two 20mm
Tubes Three 21in (1×3)
AS Four DC throwers
Machinery: Geared turbines on two shafts giving 19,000shp

Max speed: 25kts
Range: 3,500 miles at 14kts

Class Notes
These two ships were designed as anti-aircraft vessels for service in northern latitudes and as escort vessels having double decks fore and aft.

Below: HMS *Brecon*, 'Hunt' class Type 4, at sea 1943. *MoD (Navy)*

Bottom: HMS *Brissenden*, 'Hunt' class Type 4, at sea 1949. *MoD (Navy)*

Ex-Brazilian 'H' Class

Unit	Builder
Harvester (ex-*Handy*, ex-*Jurua*)	Vickers Armstrong (Barrow)
Havant (ex-*Javary*)	White
Havelock (ex-*Jutahy*)	White
Hesperus (ex-*Hearty*, ex-*Juruena*)	Thornycroft
Highlander (ex-*Jaguaribe*)	Thornycroft
Hurricane (ex-*Japarua*)	Vickers Armstrong (Barrow)

Commenced: 1939
Completed: 1940
Displacement: 1,400 tons
Length: 323ft
Breadth: 33ft
Draught: 8ft 6in
Armament: *Main* Three 4.7in
AA Seven smaller
Tubes Eight 21in (2×4)
Machinery: Geared turbines on two shafts giving 34,000shp
Max speed: 35.5kts
Fuel: 450 tons oil

Class Notes
These six destroyers arrived at a very important stage of the war, being quickly completed to act as escorts and AS vessels. All were based on the 'H' class design but upon completion lacked Y gun, a possible reason being that they were intended for use as minelayers.

Historical Notes
The body of Capt F. J. Walker CB, DSO and three bars, RN, who died 8 July 1944, was committed to the deep from HMS *Hesperus* off Liverpool Bar Light Ship. Capt Walker had been in command of Second Escort Group.

HMS *Harvester* was torpedoed on 11 March 1943 by *U432* in the western Atlantic.

HMS *Hurricane* was torpedoed on 24 December 1943 by a U-boat north-east of the Azores.

HMS *Havant* was attacked on 1 June 1940 by enemy aircraft off Dunkirk.

Early in May 1941, HMS *Hurricane* whilst at Liverpool was bombed and sunk but salvage being possible, she was raised, then refitted and was back with the fleet by January 1942.

Below: HMS *Havant* (ex-Brazilian) 'H' class, at sea 1940. *MoD (Navy)*

Ex-Turkish

Units: *Ithuriel* (ex-*Gayret*), *Inconstant* (ex-*Muavenet*)
Commenced: 1939
Completed: 1942
Builders: Vickers Armstrong (Barrow)
Displacement: 1,360 tons
2,100 tons (full load)
Length: 323ft
Breadth: 33ft
Draught: 8ft 6in

Armament: *Main* Four 4.7in (4×1 in shields)
AA Six 40mm
Tubes Eight 21in (2×4)
AS Four DC throwers
Machinery: Geared turbine on two shafts giving 34,000shp
Max speed: 35.5kts
Range: 5,000 miles at 15kts
Fuel: 450 tons oil

Class Notes

These two ships were very similar in appearance and other details to the 'Intrepid' class of the RN.

Two other ships of this class, HMS *Demir Hisar* and *Sultan Hisar*, were under construction by Denny and sailed with RN crews under the White Ensign, acting as anti-submarine escorts for their delivery voyage to Turkey. Details of the use of these vessels are given below by courtesy of the Naval Historical Branch, Ministry of Defence.

Historical notes

HMS *Ithuriel* was badly damaged by bombing in Bone Harbour 1942. It was decided not to repair her, but later she was reduced to care and maintenance and in February 1943 she was used as a base for training Italian anti-submarine personnel. She was later towed to the UK and broken up at Inverkeithing in 1945. In her short eight months of active service HMS *Ithuriel* served in force H, took part in Operation 'Pedestal', and sank the Italian submarine *Cobalto* on 12 August 1942.

After being damaged, HMS *Oribi* replaced her and took the name *Ithuriel*

Demir Hisar and *Sultan Hisar* were manned by British crews drawn from Portsmouth and Devonport respectively. They carried a full engineroom complement but only half the normal upper-deck complement, the remaining accommodation being used for suitable ratings awaiting passage. They sailed to Turkey via the Cape in two separate convoys in which they were employed as AS

Top: HMS *Ithuriel* (ex-Turkish) off Walney Island on builder's trials lacking radar, 1940. *Vickers*

Above: HMS *Inconstant* (ex-Turkish) entering Barrow on builder's trials. *Vickers*

escorts and both journeys appear to have been without incident.

HMS *Sultan Hisar* sailed from the Clyde on 22 December 1941 in company with HMS *Wivern, Active* and the armed merchant cruisers *Alaunia, Chitral, Worcestershire* and *Pretoria Castle* which were carrying service personnel. She arrived at Alexandria on 7 February 1942 where boiler cleaning, painting and minor repairs were carried out before finally sailing for Turkey on 17 February. On 19 February the *Sultan Hisar* arrived at Alexandretta where a ceremonial change of flags took place. The C-in-C Mediterranean reported that the Turkish authorities were very cordial and grateful for the safe arrival of the ship.

HMS *Demir Hisar* sailed from the Clyde on 11 January 1942 as one of the AS escorts in convoy WS15. She arrived in Capetown on 9 February with Vice-Admiral 3rd Battle Squadron (Vice-Adm W. E. C. Tait CB, MVO) temporarily embarked from HMS *Resolution*, and reached Alexandria on 14 March. She sailed again on 28 March, and C-in-C Mediterranean reported on 4 April that the *Demir Hisar* had been handed over to Turkey.

'O' ('Obdurate') Class

Unit	Builder
Obdurate	Denny
Obedient	Denny
Offa	Fairfield
Onslaught (ex-*Pathfinder*)	Fairfield
Onslow (ex-*Pakenham*)	John Brown
Opportune	Thornycroft
Oribi (ex-*Observer*)	Fairfield
Orwell	Thornycroft

Commenced: 1940 (*Opportune* and *Onslaught* 1941)
Completed: 1942 (*Oribi* and *Offa* 1941)
Displacement: 1,540 tons (*Onslow* 1,550 tons)
2,625 tons (full load)
Length: 345ft
Breadth: 35ft
Draught: 9ft
Armament: *Main* Four 4.7in
(Minelayers had three 4in at A, B, X positions)
AA Four 2pdr
Three 40mm
Tubes Eight 21in (2×4)
AS Four DC throwers, 70DCs carried

Machinery: Geared turbines on two shafts giving 40,000shp
Max speed: 34kts

Class Notes
This class were given old type 4in guns in 'lengthened shields'. They also had the distinction of being the first destroyers of the War Construction Programme. *Obdurate*, *Opportune*, *Orwell* and *Obedient* were all fitted out for minelaying.

The 'O' to 'Z' classes were designed on the hull of the 'Javelin' class and although the dimensions vary, the 'Javelins' were very 'wet' and consequently the 'O' to 'Z' classes were given more sheer from the bow to the break of the forecastle.

Historical Notes
No war losses.

Below: HMS *Obdurate*, 'O' class, at sea 1942. Notice minelaying track at stern. *MoD (Navy)*

Bottom: HMS *Offa*, 'O' class, at anchor 1945. *MoD (Navy)*

'P' ('Paladin') Class

Unit	Commenced	Completed	Builder
Pakenham (ex-Onslow)	1941	1942	Hawthorn-Leslie
Paladin	1940	1941	John Brown
Panther	1941	1942	Vickers Armstrong (Barrow)
Partridge	1941	1942	Fairfield
Pathfinder (ex-Onslaught)	1940	1941	Hawthorn-Leslie
Penn	1940	1941	Vickers Armstrong (Tyne)
Petard (ex-Persistent)	1939	1942	Vickers Armstrong (Tyne)
Porcupine	1940	1941	Vickers Armstrong (Tyne)

Displacement: 1,825 tons
2,400 tons (full load)
Length: 354ft
Breadth: 35ft
Draught: 15ft 9in
Armament: *Main* Four 4in
AA Four 40mm
Two 20mm
Tubes Eight 21in (2×4)
Machinery: Geared turbines on two shafts giving 40,000shp
Max speed: 34kts

Class Notes

These were very similar vessels to the 'O' class, having virtually the same dimensions. Y gun was mounted without a shield.

Historical Notes

HMS *Pakenham* (ex-*Onslow*) sank on 17 April 1943 after hits from Italian shore batteries on the coast of western Sicily.

HMS *Paladin* and *Petard* attacked and sank the Japanese submarine *I27* 60 miles from Addu Atoll on 12 February 1944.

HMS *Panther* sank after aircraft attack on 9 October 1943 in the Scarpanto Channel.

HMS *Partridge* was torpedoed on 18 December 1942 by a U-Boat in the western Mediterranean.

Top: HMS *Pathfinder*, 'P' class, at anchor off Plymouth breakwater. *MoD (Navy)*

Above: HMS *Penn*, 'P' class, at sea. *MoD (Navy)*

'Q' ('Queenborough') Class

Unit	Builder
Quadrant	Hawthorn-Leslie
Quail	Hawthorn-Leslie
Quality	Swan Hunter
Queenborough	Swan Hunter
Quiberon	White
Quickmatch	White
Quilliam (leader)	Hawthorn
Quentin	White

Commenced: 1940 (*Quickmatch* and *Quail* 1941)
Completed: 1942 (*Quilliam* 1941)
Displacement: 1,650 tons
2,150 tons (full load)
Length: 358ft
Breadth: 36ft
Draught: 16ft max
Armament: *Main* Four 4.7in
One 4in (aft of funnel)
AA four 40mm
Six 20mm
Tubes Eight 21in (2×4)
AS Four DC throwers

Machinery: Geared turbines on two shafts giving
40,000shp
Max speed: 34kts

Class Notes
This class had a much improved overall armament and
were slightly larger vessels than the 'O' and 'P' classes.

Historical Notes
HMS *Quail* struck a mine on 15 November 1945 and sank
in the Adriatic.

HMS *Quentin* on 2 December 1942 sank after being
struck by an aircraft-launched torpedo off Galita Island.

HMS *Quiberon* and *Quickmatch* were transferred to the
Royal Australian Navy in 1943, and *Queenborough*,
Quality, and *Quadrant* followed in 1945.

HMS *Quilliam* was transferred to the Royal
Netherlands Navy in 1945.

Below: HMS *Quickmatch*, 'Q' class, entering harbour 1942.
MoD (Navy)

Bottom: HMS *Quality*, 'Q' class, at anchor 1942. *MoD (Navy)*

'R' ('Rotherham') Class

Unit	Builder
Racehorse	John Brown
Raider	Cammell-Laird
Rapid	Cammell-Laird
Redoubt	John Brown
Relentless	John Brown
Rocket	Scotts SB
Roebuck	Scotts SB (Completed by John Brown)
Rotherham (leader)	John Brown

Commenced: 1941
Completed: 1942 (*Rapid, Rocket, Roebuck*, 1943)
Displacement: 1,735 tons (*Rotherham* 1,750 tons)
2,495 tons (full load; *Rotherham* 2,510 tons)
Length: 358ft
Breadth: 36ft
Draught: 9ft 6in

Armament: *Main* Four 4.7in
One 4in (aft of funnel)
AA Four 2pdr, Four 40mm, Six 20mm
Tubes Eight 21in (2×4)
AS Four DC throwers
Machinery: Geared turbines on two shafts giving
40,000shp
Max speed: 34kts
Fuel: 490 tons oil

Class Notes
This class represents the typical Royal Navy destroyer type of World War II. It was the first to have officers' quarters forward instead of aft.

Historical Notes
No war losses.

Above: HMS *Racehorse*, 'R' class, entering harbour 1942. *MoD (Navy)*

Left: HMS *Raider* 'R' class, leaving the fitting out basin on the River Mersey in minimum visibility conditions. The main longwire aerials are stretched from the fore to a dwarf mast at the rear of the searchlight platform, even though there is a main lattice mast.
Cammell-Laird SB

Above: HMS *Rapid*, 'R' class, leaving the Mersey after commissioning 1943. Clearly visible are the gunnery radar positioned above the director, sea boat and motorboat on the starboard main deck abreast the funnel, multiple pompoms abreast the motorboat midships, the two quadruple torpedo mountings with the searchlight platform in between, a single 20mm lower than the searchlight on both beams, twin depth charge throwers abreast of X gun and depth charge racks on the stern. *Cammell-Laird SB*

'S' ('Savage') Class

Unit	Builder
Saumarez (leader)	Hawthorn-Leslie
Savage	Hawthorn-Leslie
Scorpion (ex-*Sentinel*)	Cammell-Laird
Scourge	Cammell-Laird
Serapis	Scotts SB
Shark	Scotts SB
Success (later *Stord*)	White
Swift	White

Commenced: 1941 (*Success* 1942)
Completed: 1943
Displacement: 1,730 tons
2,535 tons (full load)
Length: 363ft
Breadth: 36ft
Draught: 10ft 6in

Armament: *Main* Four 4.7in (4×1)
(*Savage* Four 4.5in (1×2, 2×1))
AA Four 40mm
Tubes Eight 21in (2×4)
Machinery: Geared turbines on two shafts developing 40,000shp
Max speed: 36kts
Range: 2,600 miles at 22kts
Fuel: 580 tons oil

Below: HMS *Savage*, 'S' class, 1942 with a twin 4.5in turret in A position on the forecastle (prototype for the later 'Battle' classes) and 4.5in guns in single mounting at X and Y positions. *Swan Hunter*

Class Notes

This and classes to similar designs were constructed with war worthiness first and outward appearances second, yet despite this condition they were a very handsome type and their performance was second to none. They had a redesigned gunshield.

Historical Notes

HMS *Saumarez* was lost in 1946 in the Corfu Channel when she struck an Albanian mine which had been laid in an International waterway. (See HMS *Volage*)

On the fore deck of HMS *Savage* was mounted the prototype 4.5in twin turret of the 'Battle' class design.

HMS *Shark* whilst named *Svenner* and on loan to the Royal Norwegian Navy was torpedoed on 6 June 1944 off the Normandy beachhead.

HMS *Swift* struck a mine and sank off the Normandy beachhead on 24 June 1944.

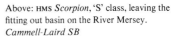

Above: HMS *Scorpion*, 'S' class, leaving the fitting out basin on the River Mersey. *Cammell-Laird SB*

Left: HMS *Scourge*, 'S' class, leaving the fitting out basin on the River Mersey. *Cammell-Laird SB*

'T' ('Troubridge') Class

Unit	Builder
Teazer	Cammell-Laird
Tenacious	Cammell-Laird
Termagant	Denny
Terpsichore	Denny
Troubridge (leader)	John Brown
Tumult	John Brown
Tuscan	Swan Hunter
Tyrian	Swan Hunter

Commenced: 1941
Completed: 1943
Displacement: 1,927 tons
2,745 tons (full load)
Length: 363ft
Breadth: 36ft
Draught: 10ft
Armament: *Main* Four 4.7in
AA Four 2pdr, Four 20mm
Tubes Eight 21in (2×4)

Machinery: Geared turbines on two shafts giving
40,000shp
Max speed: 36kts

Class Notes
Another of the very similar destroyer classes under
construction at this period. These ships were largely of all-
welded build.

HMS *Tumult* was completed with two additional fixed
tubes experimentally which were later removed.

Historical Notes
No war losses.

Below: HMS *Teazer*, 'T' class, leaving the fitting out basin on the River
Mersey under tow for builder's trials 1943. *Cammell-Laird SB*

Bottom: HMS *Tenacious*, 'T' class, steaming down Formby Channel,
River Mersey, on builder's trials. *Cammell-Laird SB*

'U' ('Ulster') Class

Unit	Com-menced	Com-pleted	Builder
Grenville (leader)	1941	1943	Swan Hunter
Ulster	1941	1943	Swan Hunter
Ulysses	1942	1943	Cammell-Laird
Undaunted	1942	1944	Cammell-Laird
Undine	1943	1943	Thornycroft
Urania	1942	1944	Vickers Armstrong (Barrow)
Urchin	1942	1943	Vickers Armstrong (Barrow)
Ursa	1942	1944	Thornycroft

Displacement: 1,710 tons
2,530 tons (full load)
Length: 362ft 9in
Breadth: 35ft 9.6in
Draught: 10ft
Armament: *Main* Four 4.7in
AA Four 40mm
Four 20mm
Tubes Eight 21in (2×4)
Machinery: Geared turbines on two shafts giving 40,000shp
Max speed: 36.75kts

Class Notes
A further class of fleet destroyers built to similar design as the preceding class. They were well built and lasting, with good sea-keeping qualities. Although the tubes were quadruple, the mountings were quintuple with the centre tube removed.

Historical Notes
No war losses.

Below: HMS *Undaunted*, 'U' class, on the Mersey for builder's trials with the searchlight platform aft of the funnel, main armament trained to port. *Cammell-Laird SB*

Bottom: HMS *Urchin*, 'U' class, passing Walney Island on builder's trials. *Vickers*

'V' ('Vigilant') Class

Unit	Builder
Hardy (leader)	John Brown
Valentine (ex-*Kempenfelt*, later HMCS *Algonquin*)	John Brown
Venus	Fairfield
Verulam	Fairfield
Vigilant	Swan Hunter
Virago	Swan Hunter
Vixen (later HMCS *Sioux*)	White
Volage	White

Commenced: 1942 (*Hardy* 1941)
Completed: 1943 (*Volage, Valentine, Vixen* 1944)
Displacement: 1,730 tons
2,530 tons (full load)
Length: 363ft
Breadth: 36ft
Draught: 13ft
Armament: *Main* Three/Four 4.7in
AA Six 40mm, Two 20mm
Tubes Eight 21in (2 × 4)
Machinery: Geared turbines on two shafts giving 40,000shp
Max speed: 36.75kts

Class Notes

This was another of the standard utility classes which were built in flotillas of eight. It should be noted that prior to 1939 the practice in planning flotillas was to have eight destroyers and one leader. Later it was decided that a flotilla would consist of eight destroyers but one of the eight would be the leader, being indistinguishable from the other ships of the class. The practice was maintained however of naming the leader after a notable captain or admiral.

Historical Notes

HMS *Hardy* whilst leader of a JW convoy, close escort was torpedoed with an acoustic torpedo by a U-boat off Bear Island, on 30 January 1944, and had to be sunk by own forces.

HMS *Volage* had her bow blown off in 1946 after striking a mine in the Corfu Channel which is an International waterway bounding Albania (see HMS *Saumarez*), but was later towed to and repaired at Malta Dockyard.

Below: HMS *Verulam*, 'V' class, at anchor 1943. *MoD (Navy)*

Bottom: HMS *Venus*, 'V' class, at anchor 1944. *MoD (Navy)*

'W' ('Wakeful') Class

Unit	Builder
Kempenfelt (leader) (ex-*Valentine*)	John Brown
Wager	John Brown
Wakeful (ex-*Zebra*)	Fairfield
Wessex (ex-*Zenith*)	Fairfield
Whelp	Hawthorn-Leslie
Whirlwind	Hawthorn-Leslie
Wizard	Vickers Armstrong (Barrow)
Wrangler	Vickers Armstrong (Barrow)

Commenced: 1942
Completed: 1944 (*Kempenfelt* 1943)
Displacement: 1,710 tons (*Kempenfelt* 1,730 tons)
2,505 tons (full load)
(*Kempenfelt* 2,525 tons full load)
Length: 363ft
Breadth: 36ft
Draught: 16ft max
Armament: *Main* Four 4.7in
AA Five 40mm, Two 20mm

Tubes Eight 21in (2 × 4)
AS Four DC throwers
Machinery: Geared turbines on two shafts giving
40,000shp
Max speed: 36.75kts

Class Notes
Similar in most respects to the preceding 'V' class. This class had a heavier main and anti-submarine armament, also a smaller main director than ships of the 'W' class.

Historical Notes
No war losses.

Below: HMS *Wrangler*, 'W' class, leaving harbour after commissioning, passing Walney Island. *Vickers*

Bottom: HMS *Wizard*, 'W' class, leaving harbour in Walney Channel for trials. *Vickers*

'Z' ('Zambesi') Class

Unit	Builder
Myngs (leader)	Vickers Armstrong (Tyne)
Zambesi	Cammell-Laird
Zealous	Cammell-laird
Zebra (ex-*Wakeful*)	Denny
Zenith (ex-*Wessex*)	Denny
Zephyr	Vickers Armstrong (Tyne)
Zest	Thornycroft
Zodiac	Thornycroft

Commenced: 1942
Completed: 1944
Displacement: 1,710 tons (*Myngs* 1,730 tons)
2,555 tons (full load; *Myngs* 2,575 tons)
Length: 363ft
Breadth: 36ft
Draught: 16ft max
Armament: *Main* Three/Four 4.5in
AA Six 40mm (*Myngs* Two 2pdr, Three 40mm)
Tubes Eight 21in (2 × 4) (*Myngs* Four 21in (1 × 4))
AS Four DC throwers
Machinery: Geared turbines on two shafts giving
40,000shp
Max speed: 34kts

Class Notes
This was the first class of 4.5in gunned destroyers, also they had a larger forward director than the 'W' class. *Zambesi* had only four tubes, and she and *Zephyr* had no Y gun, being intended for mine laying.

The 4.5in gun mounted from this class onwards including the prototype mounted on HMS *Savage*, used a 5lb heavier shell with a muzzle velocity of 200ft/sec less.

All ships from the 'O' to 'Z' classes had at least four depth charge throwers.

Historical Notes
No war losses.

Below: HMS *Zest*, 'Z' class, at anchor 1944. *MoD (Navy)*

Bottom: HMS *Zambesi*, 'Z' class, under tow leaving the fitting out basin on the River Mersey. *Cammell-Laird SB*

'C' Class

The 'C' class as built formed four flotillas grouped into four sub-classes with 'Ca', 'Ch', 'Co' and 'Cr' names. All were built to War Emergency designs and all-welded construction.

CAESAR/'Ca' GROUP

Unit	Builder
Caesar (ex-*Ranger*) (leader)	John Brown
Cambrian (ex-*Spitfire*)	Scotts SB (fitted out by John Brown)
Caprice (ex-*Swallow*)	Yarrow
Carron (ex-*Strenuous*)	Scotts SB
Carysfort	White
Cassandra (ex-*Tourmaline*)	Yarrow
Cavalier	White
Cavendish (ex-*Sibyl*)	John Brown

Commenced: 1943 (*Cambrian, Caprice, Carron* 1942)
Completed: 1944
Displacement: 1,710 tons
2,560 tons (full load)
Length: 362ft 9in
Breadth: 38ft
Draught: 10ft
Armament: *Main* Four 4.5in
AA Six 40mm
Two/Six 20mm or 2pdr

Tubes Eight 21in (2×4)
AS Four DC throwers (replaced by two Squid)
Machinery: Geared turbines on two shafts giving 40,000shp
Max speed: 36.7kts

Class Notes
Some ships were armed with a Squid in X position, this necessitated the X 4.5in gun to be suppressed and twin 40mm fitted forward of the Squid. See photograph of HMS *Carysfoot*.

Historical Notes
No war losses.

Below: HMS *Carron*, 'C' class Ca group, leaving harbour 1945. *MoD (Navy)*

Bottom: HMS *Carysfort*, 'C' class Ca group, entering harbour, 1957. Note twin Squid in place of X gun. *MoD (Navy)*

CHAPLET/'Ch' GROUP

Unit	Builder
Chaplet	Thornycroft
Charity	Thornycroft
Chequers (leader)	Scotts SB
Cheviot	Stephen
Chevron	Stephen
Chieftain (leader)	Scotts SB
Childers (ex-*Pellew*)	Denny
Chivalrous	Denny

Commenced: 1943
Completed: 1945 (*Chieftain* and *Chivalrous* 1946)
Displacement: 1,710 tons
2,560 tons (full load)
Length: 362ft 9in
Breadth: 36ft
Draught: 10ft
Armament: *Main* Four 4.5in
AA Six 40mm
Two/Six 20mm or 2pdr
Tubes Eight 21in (2×4)

AS Four DC throwers (replaced by two Squid)
Machinery: Geared turbines on two shafts giving
40,000shp
Max speed: 36.75kts

Class Notes
All to the same design as the 'Ca' group. HMS *Chaplet* and
Chieftain were fitted out as minelayers, but had one 4.5in
gun less.

Historical Notes
HMS *Charity* served in support of British and United
Nations forces from the start of the Korean War.

Below: HMS *Chaplet*, 'C' class Ch group, at sea 1945. *MoD (Navy)*

Bottom: HMS *Chieftain*, 'C' class Ch group, at sea 1946. *MoD (Navy)*

COCKADE/ 'Co' GROUP

Unit	Completed	Builder
Cockade	1945	Yarrow
Comet	1945	Yarrow
Comus	1946	Thornycroft
Concord (ex-*Corso*)	1946	Thornycroft
Consort	1946	Stephen
Constance (leader)	1944	Vickers Armstrong (Tyne)
Contest	1945	White
Cossack (leader)	1945	Vickers Armstrong (Tyne)

Commenced: 1943
Displacement: 1,710 tons
2,560 tons (full load)
Length: 362ft 9in
Breadth: 36ft
Draught: 10ft
Armament: *Main* Four 4.5in
AA Six 40mm, Two-six 20mm or 2pdr
Tubes Four 21in (1×4)
AS Four DC throwers (replaced by two Squid)
Machinery: Geared turbines on two shafts giving 40,000shp
Max speed: 36.75kts

Class Notes
All designed and built to the same specifications as the 'Ch' group. HMS *Comet* and *Contest* were minelayers and lacked the sternmost 4.5in gun. (See photograph of HMS *Contest*).

Historical Notes
HMS *Concord* and *Consort* took part in the 'Yangtse Incident' 1949. Later HMS *Cockade, Comus, Concord, Consort, Constance* and *Cossack* were a part of the Royal Naval supporting forces to the United Nations armies in Korea.

Left: HMS *Contest*, 'C' class Co group, 1957. Note minelaying rails with X and Y guns suppressed. *MoD (Navy)*

Below: HMS *Concord*, 'C' class Co group, at sea 1946. Note walkways above tubes. *MoD (Navy)*

CRESCENT/ 'Cr' GROUP

Unit	Commenced	Completed	Builder
Creole	1944	1946	White
Crescent (leader)	1943	1945	John Brown
Crispin (ex-*Craccher*)	1944	1946	White
Cromwell (ex-*Cretan*)	1943	1945	Scotts SB
Crown	1944	1947	Scotts SB
Croziers	1944	1945	Yarrow
Crusader (leader)	1943	1945	John Brown
Crystal	1944	1946	Yarrow

Displacement: 1,710 tons
2,560 tons (full load)
Length: 362ft 9in
Breadth: 36ft
Draught: 10ft
Armament: *Main* Four 4.5in
AA Six 40mm, Two-six 20mm
Tubes Four 21in (1×4)
AS Four DC throwers (replaced by Squid)

Machinery: Geared turbines on two shafts giving 40,000shp
Max speed: 36kts

Class Notes
These, the final eight of the 1943 'C' class, were to the same designs as the 'Ca' group, and were of all-welded construction.

Historical Notes
HMS *Crown* never saw service in the Royal Navy, for although launched with that name, she was, upon completion, commissioned into the Royal Norwegian Navy.

Below: HMS *Creole*, 'C' class Cr group, at anchor 1946. *MoD (Navy)*

Bottom: HMS *Crispin*, 'C' class Cr group, at anchor 1946. *MoD (Navy)*

'Battle' Class

GROUP 1

Unit	Commenced	Completed	Builder	Unit	Commenced	Completed	Builder
Barfleur (leader)	1942	1944	Swan Hunter	*Hogue*	1943	1945	Cammell-Laird
				Lagos	1943	1945	Cammell-Laird
Camperdown	1942	1945	Fairfield	*St Kitts*	1943	1946	Swan Hunter
Finisterre	1942	1945	Fairfield	*Trafalgar* (leader)	1943	1945	Swan Hunter
Gabbard	1944	1946	Swan Hunter				

GROUP II

Unit	Commenced	Completed	Builder	Unit	Commenced	Completed	Builder
Armada (leader)	1942	1945	Hawthorn-Leslie	*St James* (leader)	1943	1946	Fairfield
Cadiz	1943	1946	Fairfield	*Sluys*	1943	1946	Cammell-Laird
Gravelines	1943	1946	Cammell-Laird	*Solebay* (leader)	1943	1945	Hawthorn-Leslie
Saintes (leader)	1943	1946	Hawthorn-Leslie	*Vigo*	1943	1946	Fairfield

Displacement: 2,315 tons (Group I)
2,325 tons (Group II)
3,250 tons (Group I full load)
3,360 tons (Group II full load)
Length: 379ft
Breadth: 40ft
Draught: 12ft 9in
Armament: *Main* Four 4.5in (2×2 in turrets)
AA Ten 40mm
Tubes Eight 21in (2×4)
AS Two DC throwers (replaced by one Squid)
Machinery: Geared turbines on two shafts giving
50,000shp
Max speed: 35.75kts

Class Notes
This class was intended for service in the Tropics and the Pacific Theatre. They had the main armament forward and the anti-aircraft and light weapons aft of the funnel. The turrets were powered and the 4.5in guns had 85° elevation. The AA weapons were all mounted clear of the main deck. Additionally a single 40mm Bofors was positioned aft of B turret in front of the bridge.

HMS *Saintes* was the trials vessel for the prototype 4.5in twin turret for the 'Daring' class.

Group I ships mounted a 4in for star shell aft of the funnel. These were not utility ships and took longer to build.

Below: HMS *Gabbard*, 'Battle' class group 1, at anchor 1946.
MoD (Navy)

Top: HMS *Hogue*, 'Battle' class group 1, at sea with all armament and director trained to starboard. *Cammell-Laird SB*

Above: HMS *Sluys*, 'Battle' class group 2, leaving harbour 1946. Note 4.5in aft of funnel and 40mm aft of the B turret before the bridge. *MoD (Navy)*

Later 'Battle' Class

Unit	Com-menced	Com-pleted	Builder
Agincourt (leader)	1943	1947	Hawthorn-Leslie
Aisne	1943	1947	Vickers Armstrong (Tyne)
Alamein (leader)	1944	1948	Hawthorn-Leslie
Barrosa	1943	1947	John Brown
Corunna (leader)	1944	1947	Swan Hunter
Dunkirk	1944	1946	Stephen
Jutland (ex-*Malplaquet*) (leader)	1944	1947	Stephen
Matapan	1944	1947	John Brown

Displacement: 2,640 tons (2,480 tons leaders) 3,315 tons (full load) (3,375 tons leaders full load)
Armament: *Main* Five 4.5in (2×2, 1×1)
AA Eight 40mm
Tubes Ten 21in (2×5)
AS One triple Squid
Machinery: Geared turbines on two shafts giving 50,000shp
Max speed: 35.75kts

Below: HMS *Barrosa*, later 'Battle' class, entering harbour 1947. *MoD (Navy)*

Above: HMS *Corunna*, later 'Battle' class, at sea 1947. *MoD (Navy)*

Unit	Builder
Albuera	Vickers Armstrong (Tyne)
Belleisle	Fairfield
Mons	Hawthorn-Leslie
Namur*	Cammell-Laird
Navarino	Cammell-Laird
Omdurman	Fairfield
Oudenarde*	Swan Hunter
Poictiers	Hawthorn-Leslie
River Plate	Swan Hunter
St Lucia	Stephen
San Domingo	Cammell-Laird
Somme	Cammell-Laird
Talavera	Clydebank
Trincomalee	Clydebank
Waterloo	Fairfield
Vimiera	Not allocated
Ypres	Not allocated

Class Notes

A very fine design of destroyer being an improved version of the 'Battle' class with greater firepower. An ideal recognition point for this class is the US style of 'pagoda battleship type' director just forward of the flag deck. None of this class saw World War II service. All ships mounted a single 4.5in gun in shield aft of the funnel.

Historical Notes

The following ships of both 'Battle' classes were in varying states of completion, some just a name on an order book, some on the slips, and some launched and fitting-out when the war ended. All were cancelled, broken up or scrapped.

*Namur and *Oudenarde* were actually launched and made seaworthy being expended later as targets.

Ex-German

'NARVIK' CLASS

Unit: *Nonsuch* (ex-*Z38*)
Commenced: 1942
Completed: 1943
Builder: Deschimag
Displacement: 2,650 tons (full load)
Length: 403ft 6in
Breadth: 38ft 6in
Draught: 9ft 6in
Armament: *Main* Five 5.9in
AA Six 37mm, 16 20mm

Tubes Eight 21in
Machinery: Geared turbines on two shafts giving 70,000shp
Max speed: 35.5kts
Fuel: 800 tons oil

Below: HMS *Nonsuch* (ex-German) 'Narvik' class, in harbour under German flag, 1944. *Real Photographs*

'MAASS' CLASS

Unit: *Z4* (ex-*Richard Beitzon*), *Z10* (ex-*Hans Lady*)
Commenced: 1935
Completed: 1941
Builder: *Z4* Deutsche werke
Z10 Deschimag
Displacement: 1,625 tons
2,360 tons (full load)
Length: 382ft
Breadth: 37ft 6in
Draught: 9ft 6in
Armament: *Main* Five 5in
AA Eight 37mm, 12 20mm
Tubes Eight 21in
Machinery: Geared turbines on two shafts giving
50,000shp
Max speed: 36kts

Class Notes
These three ex-German destroyers were allocated to the Royal Navy as reparations after the war's end. They were taken to Portsmouth for evaluation and all three were made seaworthy — *Z38* having a damaged hull and needing refit, *Z10* had minor defects and *Z4* had been badly damaged by a near miss from a bomb that took five months to repair. All carried 60 mines.

Z38 was commissioned as HMS *Nonsuch*, *Z10* and *Z4* were not used.

Z38 was one of the 'Narvik' class of destroyer built after the Battle of Narvik when the RN 'H' class gave battle to the prewar German destroyers in Narvik Fjord.

Z4 and *Z10* were of the first German class to mount quadruple torpedo tubes in two mountings.

Although all three of these ships were on the Navy list, only HMS *Nonsuch* saw service under the White Ensign, being used as an air target towing vessel, being broken up in 1949. The photograph of HMS *Nonsuch* was taken prior to her RN service.

'Weapon' Class

Unit	Builder
Battleaxe (leader)	Yarrow
Broadsword (leader)	Yarrow
Crossbow	Thornycroft
Scorpion (ex-*Tomahawk*, ex-*Centaur*)	White

Commenced: 1944
Completed: 1947 (*Broadsword* and *Crossbow* 1948)
Displacement: 2,000 tons
2,835 tons (full load)
Length; 365ft
Breadth: 38ft
Draught: 12ft 9in
Armament: *Main* Four 4in
AA Four 40mm
Tubes Ten 21in (2 × 5)
AS 15 DCs carried, Two Squid
Machinery: Geared turbines on two shafts giving
40,000shp
Max speed: 34kts

Class Notes
This class was composed of destroyers intended for fleet use but altered at design stage for anti-submarine work, and thus only mounted four instead of six 4in guns. In the first two ships the 4in guns were in A and X positions, in the latter two, in A and B positions; all the 4in guns were in shields.

These were the first two-funnelled destroyers to be built since the 'Tribals' of 1939 and the only completed units from a planned total of 20.

The outline was similar to the next class, the 'Darings'. The fore funnel was built inside the lattice fore mast and all were fitted as leaders. This class design was an enlargement of the 'Hunt' Type IV.

Below: HMS *Broadsword*, 'Weapon' class, at anchor, 1948.
MoD (Navy)

Historical Notes

HMS *Carronade* of this class was launched but not completed.

    HMS *Scorpion* was the destroyer chosen to be the trials ship for the Limbo anti-submarine weapon.

Left: HMS *Crossbow*, 'Weapon' class, entering harbour, 1959. *MoD (Navy)*

'Daring' Class

Unit	Com- menced	Com- pleted	Builder
Dainty	1945	1953	White
Daring	1945	1952	Swan Hunter
Decoy (ex-*Dragon*)	1946	1953	Yarrow
Defender (ex-*Dogstar*)	1949	1952	Stephen
Delight (ex-*Disdain*, ex-*Ypres*)	1946	1953	Fairfield
Diamond	1947	1954	John Brown
Diana (ex-*Druid*)	1947	1954	Yarrow
Duchess	1948	1952	Thornycroft

Displacement: 2,610 tons
3,600 tons (full load)
Length: 390ft
Breadth: 43ft
Draught: 12ft 9in
Armament: *Main* Six 4.5in (3 × 2 in turrets)
AA Six 40mm
Tubes Ten 21in (2 × 5)

AS Squid
Machinery: Geared turbines on two shafts giving 54,000shp
Max speed: 34.75kts

Class Notes

This class is a partial design improvement on the 'Battle' and 'Weapon' classes, and of all-welded construction. A recognition feature is the bridge of new design, also the 4.5in gun turrets. The fore funnel is partly built into and concealed by the fore mast.

    All classed as leaders, 16 were planned.

    The 'Daring' class destroyers have been described as 'super destroyers' and even as 'ultralight cruisers'. Up to the year 1954, they were the largest destroyers in size and tonnage in the RN.

Below: HMS *'Daring'*, 'Daring' class, at sea 1952. Note smoke from fore-funnel. *MoD (Navy)*

Above: HMS *Delight*, 'Daring' class, at anchor 1953. *MoD (Navy)*

'County' Class

Unit	Com-menced	Com-pleted	Builder
Antrim	1966	1971	Fairfield
Devonshire	1959	1962	Cammell-Laird
Fife	1962	1966	Vickers Armstrong (Tyne)
Glamorgan	1962	1966	Fairfield
Hampshire	1959	1963	John Brown (Clyde)
Kent	1960	1963	Harland & Wolff
London	1960	1963	Swan Hunter
Norfolk	1966	1970	Swan Hunter

Displacement: 5,200 tons
6,200 tons (full load)
Length: 520ft 6in
Breadth: 54ft
Draught: 20ft
Armament: *Main* Four 4.5in (2 × 2 in turrets)
AA Two 20mm
Missiles Two quadruple Seacat, One Seaslug (twin mounting)
Tubes Three 12.75in (either beam if fitted)
Machinery: Combined steam and gas, COSAG, on two shafts giving 60,000shp

Max speed: 32.5kts
Range: 3,500 miles at 28kts

Class Notes
These eight ships when built embodied the latest technological developments enabling them to fight in a nuclear war. Armed with Seaslug and Seacat surface-to-surface and surface-to-air missiles, the 'County' class has a powerful anti-ship armament not forgetting the four 4.5in guns which are semi-automatic, dual-purpose and have a good angle of elevation. Anti-submarine warfare is taken care of by the ship's flight of one or two Wessex helicopters and the AS torpedoes, which are also light enough for helicopter use and carry an 88lb warhead. Other defensive equipment includes two eight-barrelled Corvus chaff-dischargers which dispense a screen of chaff to obscure the ship to enemy missiles. The launchers are mounted port and starboard of the fore funnel. The engine room has one AEI and one G6 turbine on each shaft. The machinery is similar to that on the Type 81 'Tribal' class frigates.

Below: HMS *Devonshire*, 'County' class, on builder's trials under the red ensign, 1962. *MoD (Navy)*

Type 82

Unit: *Bristol*
Builder: Associated Shipbuilders, Wallesend-on-Tyne
Commenced: Nov 1967
Completed: Dec 1972
Displacement: 5,650 tons
6,750 tons (full load)
Length: 508ft
Breadth: 55ft
Draught: 22ft 6in
Armament: *Main* One Sea Dart (twin mounting in Y position)
One 4.5in (turret in A position)
AA Two 20mm (2 × 1)
AS Ikara aft A position, Limbo Mk 10 (One three-barrel mounting)

Machinery: COSAG on two shafts developing 74,600shp
Max speed: 28kts
Range: 5,000nm at 18kts
Helicopter: Deck suitable for Wasp, no hangar

Class Notes

HMS *Bristol* is the only completed example of an aircraft carrier escort vessel. A total of eight was proposed but only this example, ordered in October 1966, was commissioned. She has stabilisers and all her compartments are air conditioned. She is the only three-funnelled ship in the Royal Navy.

Below: HMS *Bristol*, Type 82, at sea on builder's trials. 1975. *MoD (Navy)*

Type 42

Unit	Commenced	Completed	Builder
Birmingham	1971	1976	Cammell-Laird
Cardiff	1971	1978	Vickers-Barrow
Coventry	1972	1978	Cammell-Laird
Exeter	1978		Swan Hunter
Glasgow	1972	1978	Swan Hunter
Liverpool	1978	1982	Cammell-Laird
Newcastle	1972	1978	Swan Hunter
Nottingham	1978		Vosper Thornycroft
Sheffield	1970	1974	Vickers-Barrow
Southampton	1978		Vosper Thornycroft

Displacement: 3,150 tons
4,100 tons (full load)
Length: 410ft
Breadth: 46ft
Draught: 19ft
Armament: *Main* Twin Sea Dart Mk 30 (in B position)
One 4.5in (turret in A position)
AA Two 20mm (2×1)
Tubes Six 12.75in AS (2×3 abreast of after director)
Machinery: COGOG on two shafts giving 50,000 and 8,000shp
Max speed: 28kts
Range: 650nm at 30kts
4,500nm at 18kts
Helicopter: One Lynx armed with Sea Skua

Class Notes

A simpler design warship than HMS *Bristol*, but in general based on the Type 82 specification. The high speed Olympus turbines are not coupled to the Tyne turbines which are only used for cruising. Each shaft has a five-bladed variable pitch propeller. HMS *Sheffield* was ordered in November 1968.

The 4.5in gun has depression of 10° and elevation of 55° from the horizontal, with 25 rounds/barrel/min. The weight of the shell (HE charge) is 21kg, and its range

Top left: HMS *Sheffield*, 'Towns' class, leaving Vickers basin for sea trials. *Vickers*

Centre left: HMS *Birmingham*, 'Towns' class, at sea. *MoD (Navy)*

Bottom left: HMS *Newcastle*, 'Towns' class, at sea under the red ensign for builder's trials. *MoD (Navy)*

22km. This weapon is developed from the Abbot SP gun.

The Sea Dart missile is propelled by a solid fuel booster engine and a ramjet sustainer with radar guidance. The missile is semi-active radar homed, with an HE warhead and a range of 25nm.

The Sea Skua missile is propelled by solid fuel rocket and guided by radar and/or radio control with an estimated maximum effective range of 6nm and carries an HE warhead of 45lb.

The 12.75in diameter torpedo is an active and/or acoustic homing weapon, mainly for air to surface/sub-surface warfare.

Improved Type 42

Unit	Commenced	Builder
Manchester	1979	Vickers-Barrow
Gloucester	1979	Vosper Thornycroft
York	1980	Swan Hunter
Edinburgh	1980	Cammell Laird

Displacement: 4,500 tons (deep load)
Length: 463ft
Breadth: 49ft
Draught: 13.5ft
Armament: *Main* Twin Sea Dart Mk 30 (in B position)
AA 20mm Mk 7A (2×1 on bridge deck)
DP One 4.5in turret (in A position)
Tubes Six Mk 32 AS (2×3 abreast of after director above main deck level)
Machinery: COGOG Rolls-Royce Olympus gas turbines developing 50,000shp and two RM1A gas turbines for cruising, developing 5,200shp, to two shafts with controllable pitch propellers

Speed: 28kts
Helicopter: One Lynx

Class Notes
The design of these four ships has been called the 'Stretched Type 42'. The stretching gives a longer and beamier hull with better sea keeping ability plus additional hull and deck space for the increase in complement and a probable heavier weapon outfit to that listed above. The vessels also carry two Corvus Chaff dispensers.

Below: A proposal to improve the Type 42s led to the 'Stretched' version. The line drawing shows the intended layout and (bottom) HMS *Manchester*, the first of the type, is seen at its launch on 24 November 1980. *Vickers*

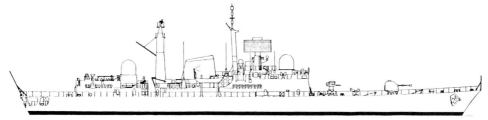

Appendices
1 Destroyer Armament

Guns

Calibre	Muzzle Velocity (ft/sec)	Projectile weight	Notes
6in	2,400	100lb	As mounted on HMS *Swift* 1917.
4.7in DP	3,000	55-65lb	QF — Mounted on the majority of classes from the Thornycroft leaders of 1917.
4.5in DP	3,750	60lb	QF — First mounted in the 'Z' class 1943. In the latest classes are automatic.
4in DP	2,300	31lb or 25lb	QF — The main armament of destroyers from the 'F' class 1908 and for many vessels in World War 2.
3in or 12pdr	2,500	12-16lb	Mounted on the first 'A' to 'E' classes and usually referred to as 12-pounders.
2.24in	1,740	6lb	As above and known as 6-pounders.
'Pom-Poms'	2,000	2lb	First effectively used in the Boer War on land. Fully automatic action.
40mm Bofors	2,500	4.5lb	One of the best light AA pieces designed. Fully automatic action.
20mm Oerlikon	2,725	125g	A heavy machine gun weapon for short range AA work.
5in Vickers	2,520	2.19oz	Heavy machine gun type. Chiefly for short range AA work.

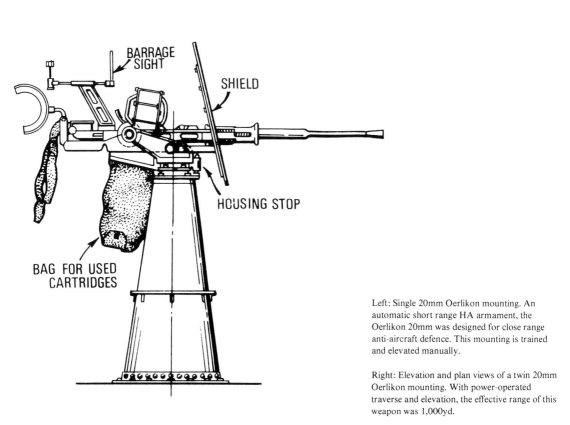

BARRAGE SIGHT

SHIELD

HOUSING STOP

BAG FOR USED CARTRIDGES

Left: Single 20mm Oerlikon mounting. An automatic short range HA armament, the Oerlikon 20mm was designed for close range anti-aircraft defence. This mounting is trained and elevated manually.

Right: Elevation and plan views of a twin 20mm Oerlikon mounting. With power-operated traverse and elevation, the effective range of this weapon was 1,000yd.

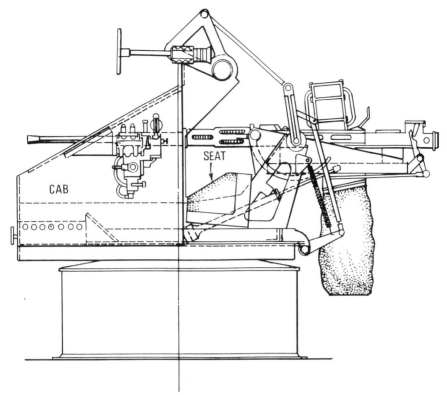

ELEVATION OF GUNLAYERS SIDE OF TWIN MOUNTING

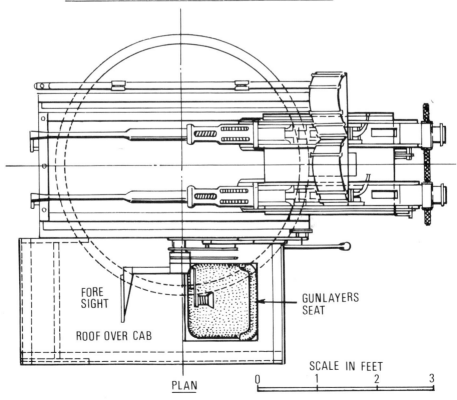

CAB

SEAT

FORE
SIGHT

ROOF OVER CAB

GUNLAYERS
SEAT

PLAN

SCALE IN FEET

0   1   2   3

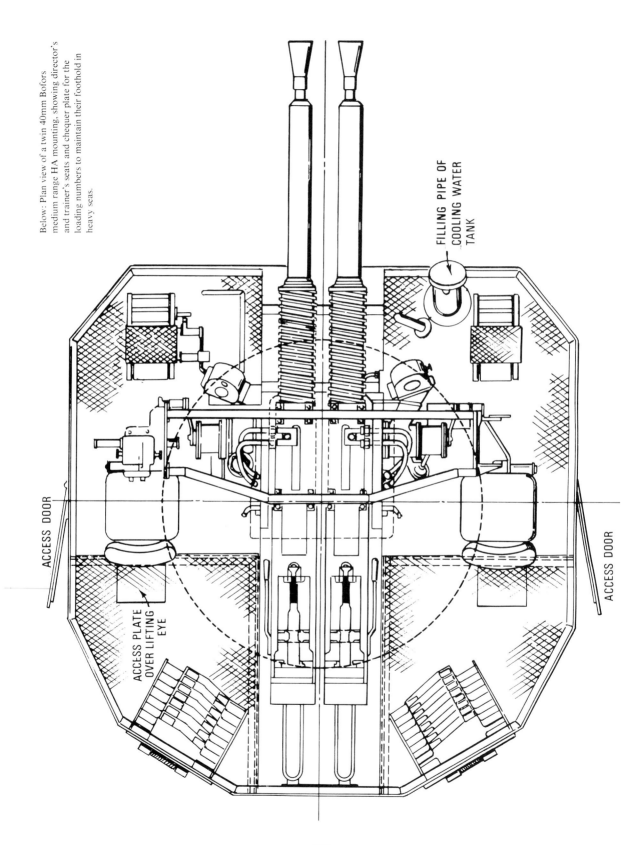

Below: Plan view of a twin 40mm Bofors medium range HA mounting, showing director's and trainer's seats and chequer plate for the loading numbers to maintain their foothold in heavy seas.

FILLING PIPE OF COOLING WATER TANK

ACCESS DOOR

ACCESS DOOR

ACCESS PLATE OVER LIFTING EYE

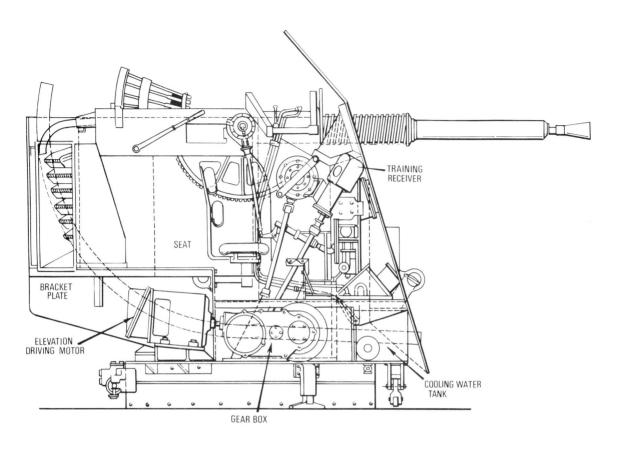

TRAINING
RECEIVER

SEAT

BRACKET
PLATE

ELEVATION
DRIVING MOTOR

GEAR BOX

COOLING WATER
TANK

Above: Elevation of a twin 40mm Bofors. This mounting was a logical extension of the single piece seen below, with the advantage of complete automation for elevation and training, but full local control independent of the director when necessary.

Below: Single 40mm Bofors mounting. Power-operated for training and elevation, local control is built in to this weapon.

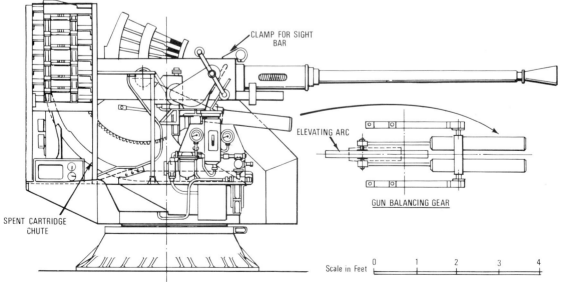

CLAMP FOR SIGHT
BAR

ELEVATING ARC

GUN BALANCING GEAR

SPENT CARTRIDGE
CHUTE

Scale in Feet 0 1 2 3 4

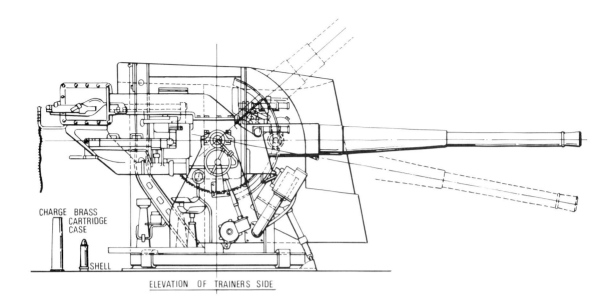

CHARGE BRASS
CARTRIDGE
CASE

SHELL

ELEVATION OF TRAINERS SIDE

Above: 4.7in QF Mk IX gun on the CP Mk XVIII mounting. It has an elevation of 40° and depression of 10°. The gun itself is built up of three forgings — the gun tube (called the 'A' tube), the jacket and the breech ring.

Below: Plan view of the 4.7in DP gun. This drawing shows the mounting as fitted to the 'Javelin' class destroyers and the instrumentation for training, elevation and fuse setting in either local or director control.

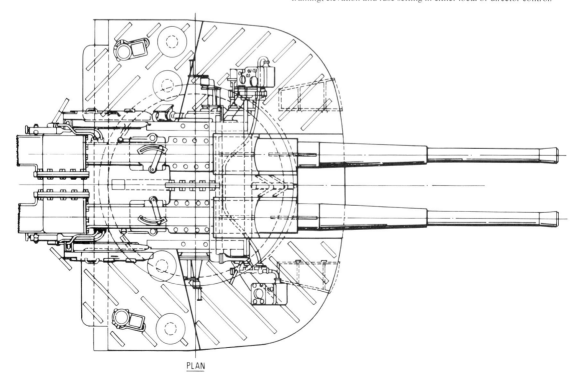

PLAN

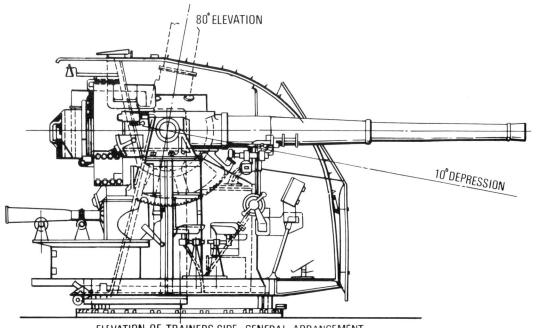

80° ELEVATION

10° DEPRESSION

ELEVATION OF TRAINERS SIDE GENERAL ARRANGEMENT

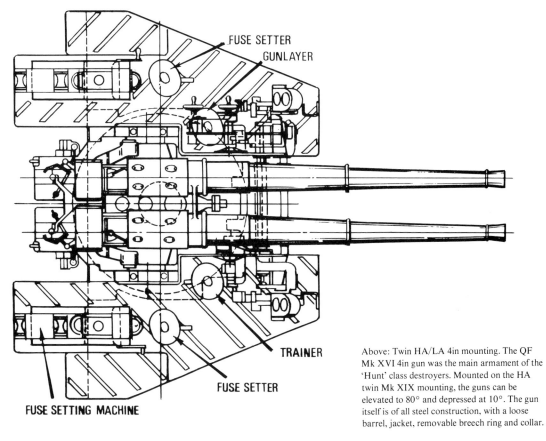

FUSE SETTER

GUNLAYER

TRAINER

FUSE SETTER

FUSE SETTING MACHINE

Above: Twin HA/LA 4in mounting. The QF
Mk XVI 4in gun was the main armament of the
'Hunt' class destroyers. Mounted on the HA
twin Mk XIX mounting, the guns can be
elevated to 80° and depressed at 10°. The gun
itself is of all steel construction, with a loose
barrel, jacket, removable breech ring and collar.

Anti-Submarine Weapons

Name	Description	Notes
Name	*Description*	*Notes*
Depth Charge	300lb charge in an oil drum shaped cylindrical container. Detonates at a preset depth. In WW2 a cast iron ballast weight was fitted to give a fast sink rate.	Brought into service between 1914-18. Either fired abeam from a mortar like thrower, or released from a chute by gravity.
Hedgehog	24 spigot type bombs mounted upon a rectangular cradle, forward of the bridge, and fired ahead on a given command, in an oval pattern; the bombs had a 37lb charge with contact fuse.	In service from 1942 and later. Range: one cable; effective down to 1,250ft
Squid	Two, three of four bombs fired from barrels, similar to the mortar principle. Bombs of 500lb charge.	Not in service in the RN today. Range three cables.
Limbo Mk 10	AS mortar with all round coverage, has three barrels. Maximum effective range of five cables.	In service today. Introduced in the early 1960s as an improved Squid.

Below: Practice drill at a depth charge thrower on board HMS *Anthony* ('A' class) during the interwar years. *IWM*

114

Guided Missiles

Name	Description	Notes
Seaslug	Medium range AA missile with surface-to-surface capability. 15 miles range, 500ft-50,000ft altitude.	Used in the 'County' class, after trials in HMS *Girdle Ness*. Mk I and II fitted.
Sea Dart	Medium range DP missile up to 25 miles and between 100ft-60,000ft altitude.	Fitted in HMS *Bristol* and the Type 42 'Sheffield' class.
Seacat	Short range AA missile with DP possibility, range/height 13,000ft.	Fitted in the majority of RN fighting ships.
Sea Skua	This is a comparatively new missile launched from the helicopter for anti-ship use.	
Harpoon	A tactical surface-to-surface missile system with a range of 55-120nm. Missile particulars are: length 15ft weight 1,470lb, speed Mach 0.9, warhead 500lb HE or nuclear. Propulsion is by solid fuel rocket motor and guidance is by radar.	Likely to be fitted to the Type 42s.

Below: Sea Slug. This medium range ship-to-air missile is fitted in the 'County' class guided missile destroyers, in this case HMS *Kent*. It has four solid propellant boosters which jettison after burn-out. It is guided by a beam riding system from radar Type 901. *MoD (Navy)*

Right: Sea Dart. This medium range ship-to-air missile is propelled by ramjets. It also has an anti-ship capability. *MoD (Navy)*

Below: Seacat. A highly efficient close range anti-aircraft missile which can be used in a surface-to-surface role. Guidance is by radio control with solid fuel propulsion. *MoD (Navy)*

Above right: Lynx helicopter with two Mk 44/46 torpedoes. Developed for AS and other duties the Lynx carries a variety of armament including the Sea Skua semi-active homing missile. The Lynx is carried by the Type 42s. *Fleet Air Arm Museum*

Right: Wasp helicopter used in conjunction with the Type 81s normally armed with two Mk 44/46 torpedoes. *Fleet Air Arm Museum*

Right: The Sea King helicopter carries a variety of equipment including sonar, search radar and up to four Mk 44 torpedoes or depth charges. *Fleet Air Arm Museum*

Below: Wessex helicopter, normally carried on 'County' class destroyers. *Fleet Air Arm Museum*

Torpedoes

Diameter	Description	Notes
14in	Used in the earliest TBDs up to the Admiralty 'S' Class.	Either the tube mounting or ship, or both had to be 'trained' for the torpedo to bear directly at the target.
18in	Used in the 'B' to 'F' classes.	
21in	Classes after the 'S' class up to the 'County' class of 1960.	
12.75in	This is a recent type of torpedo being electrically propelled and with a warhead of only 88lb. It is much shorter than the 21in torpedo and is ideal for helicopter use.	Provided for in the 'County' and later classes.

Below: 21in torpedo test firing from HMS *Broke* c1914. *Vickers*

119

Above: 18in torpedo less pistol arming device on warhead. *Vickers*   Below: 21in torpedo clearing the deck of a destroyer into the sea. *IWM*

2 Destroyer Builders in the UK

Cammell-Laird & Co (Shipbuilders and Engineers) Ltd, Birkenhead, Cheshire.

John Brown & Co (Shipbuilders and Engineers) Ltd, Clydebank, Glasgow.

Wm Denny & Bros Ltd, Dumbarton.

The Fairfield Shipbuilding & Engineering Co Ltd, Govan, Glasgow.

Harland & Wolff Ltd, Belfast, Glasgow and Govan.

R. & W. Hawthorn Leslie & Co Ltd, Hebburn-on-Tyne.

Scotts Shipbuilding & Engineering Co Ltd (Greenock).

Smiths Dock Co Ltd, South Bank on Tees.

Alex, Stephen & Sons Ltd (Linthouse, Govan, Glasgow).

Swan, Hunter & Wigham Richardson Ltd, Wallsend-on-Tyne.

John I. Thornycroft & Co Ltd, Woolston, Southampton.

Vickers-Armstrong, Naval Yard, Barrow-in-Furness, Lancashire.

Vickers-Armstrong, Naval Yard, High Walker, Newcastle-on-Tyne, and Palmers Hebburn Co Ltd.

J. Samuel White & Co Ltd, Cowes.

Yarrow & Co Ltd, Scotstoun, Glasgow.

Also used: Doxford (Sunderland); Earle (Hull); Harland and Wolff (Clyde); Inglis (Clyde); Thames Iron Works (Blackwall); Beardmore (Clyde).

3 Details of Torpedo Catchers and Torpedo Destroyers

Unit	Length (ft)	Speed (kts)	Armament	Completed	Unit	Length (ft)	Speed (kts)	Armament	Completed
Alarm	230	17	2-12pdr and 4 smallbore	1892	*Leda*	230	17	2-12pdr and 4 smallbore	1892
Antelope	230	17	2-12pdr and 4 smallbore	c1892	*Niger*	230	17	2-12pdr and 4 smallbore	1892
Assaye	230	15	2-12pdr and 4 smallbore	1891	*Onyx*	230	17	2-12pdr and 4 smallbore	1892
Barracouta	220	14	6-12pdr and 4 smallbore	1889	*Peassey*	230	15	2-12pdr and 4 smallbore	1890
Barrossa	220	14	6-12pdr and 4 smallbore	1889	*Rattlesnake*	200	17.5	1-12pdr and 6 smallbore	1886
Blanche	220	14	6-12pdr and 4 smallbore	1889	*Salamander*	230	15	2-12pdr and 4 smallbore	1889
Blonde	230	14	6-12pdr and 4 smallbore	1889	*Sandfly*	200	?	6 smallbore	1887
Boomerang	230	15	2-12pdr and 4 smallbore	1892	*Scout*	220	12	4-12pdr and 8 smallbore and 1 submerged TT	1885
Circe	230	17	2-12pdr and 4 smallbore	1892					
Curlew	195	10	1-6in and 3-4.7in	1885	*Seagull*	230	15	2-12pdr and 4 smallbore	1889
Dryad	250	16.5	2-12pdr and 4 smallbore	1890	*Sharpshooter*	230	18	2-12pdr and 4 smallbore	1888
Fearless	220	12	4-12pdr and 8 smallbore 1 submerged TT	1886	*Sheldrake*	230	15	2-12pdr and 4 smallbore	1889
					Skipjack	230	15	2-12pdr and 4 smallbore	1889
Gleaner	230	15	2-12pdr and 4 smallbore	1890	*Spanker*	230	15	2-12pdr and 4 smallbore	1889
Gossamer	230	15	2-12pdr and 4 smallbore	1890	*Speedwell*	230	15	2-12pdr and 4 smallbore	1889
Grasshopper	200	?	6 smallbore	1887	*Spider*	200	?	1-12pdr and 6 smallbore	1887
Halcyon	250	16.5	2-12pdr and 4 smallbore	c1890					
Harrier	250	16.5	2-12pdr and 4 smallbore	c1890					
Hazard	250	16.5	2-12pdr and 4 smallbore	c1890					
Hebe	230	17	2-12pdr and 4 smallbore	1892					
Hussar	250	16.5	2-12pdr and 4 smallbore	c1890					
Jason	230	17	2-12pdr and 4 smallbore	1892					
Jaseur	230	17	2-12pdr and 4 smallbore	1892					
Karrakatta	230	15	2-12pdr and 4 smallbore	1889					
Landrail	195	10	1-6in and 3-4.7in	1886					

4 Statement of Losses of HM Destroyers and Torpedo Boats

Torpedo Boats lost 1914-18

HMTB9 (ex-HMTB *Grasshopper*) was lost by collision in the North Sea, 24 July 1916.

HMTB10 (ex-HMTB *Greenfly*) was torpedoed by a U-boat in the North Sea 10 June 1915.

HMTB11 (ex-HMTB *Moth*) struck a mine off the east coast 7 March 1916.

HMTB12 (ex-HMTB *Mayfly*) was torpedoed by a U-boat in the North Sea on 10 June 1915.

HMTB13 was lost by collision in the North Sea, 28 January 1916.

HMTB24 was wrecked off Dover Harbour breakwater, 28 January 1917.

HMTB046 foundered in a storm in the eastern Mediterranean on 27 December 1915.

HMTB064 was wrecked in the Agean sea on 21 March 1915.

HMTB90 capsized in a storm off Gibraltar on 25 April 1918.

HMTB96 collided with a Mercantile Fleet Auxiliary off Gibraltar on 1 November 1915.

HMTB 17 was lost by collision in the English Channel; 10 June 1917.

Summary
Foundered: 4
Collision: 4
Mined: 1
Torpedoed: 2
Total: 11

At the cessation of hostilities in 1918 HMTB 1-8, 14-23, 25-36 and 116 were still in service.

Torpedo Boat Destroyers lost 1914-18

Ardent, Ariel, Arno, Attack, Bittern, Boxer, Cheerful, Comet, Contest, Coquette, Derwent, Eden, Erne, Fairy, Falcon, Flirt, Fortune, Foyle, Goldfinch, Gurkha, Hoste, Itchen, Kale, Laforey, Lassoo, Lightning, Louis, Lynx, Maori, Marmion, Mary Rose, Medusa, Myrmidon, Narborough, Negro, Nessus, Nestor, Nomad, North Star, Nubian*, Opal, Paragon, Partridge, Pheasant, Phoenix, Pincher, Racoon, Recruit (1), Recruit (2), Scott, Setter, Shark, Simoon, Sparrowhawk, Staunch, Strongbow, Success, Surprise, Tipperary, Tornado, Torrent, Turbulent, Ulleswater, Ulysses, Vehement, Velox, Vittoria**, Wolverine, Zulu*.

*Nubian and *Zulu* were only counted as one loss, see page 22.
**Vittoria was not lost during the war, see page 46.

Summary
Mined: 22
Sunk by U-boat: 10 (see details below)
Rammed: 2
Surface action: 13
Collision: 14
Wrecked: 8
Total: 69

RN destroyers lost by enemy submarine attack, 1914-18

Attacked	*By*	*Nationality*
Attack	*UC-34*	German
Comet	Unknown	Austrian
Contest	Unknown	German
Fairy	*UC-75*	German
Itchen	*U-99*	German
Phoenix	*U-XXVII*	Austrian
Recruit (1)	Unknown	German
Recruit (2)	*UB-16*	German
Scott	*UC-17*	German
Staunch	*UC-38*	German
Ulleswater	Unknown	German

Lassoo, Surprise, Tornado and *Torrent* are now known to have sunk after striking a mine, and not as a result of submarine attack.

RN Destroyers Lost 1939-45

Acasta, Achates, Acheron, Afridi, Airedale, Aldenham, Ardent, Basilisk, Bath, Bedouin, Belmont, Berkeley, Beverley, Blanche, Blean, Boadicea, Brazen, Broadwater, Broke, Campbeltown, Cameron, Codrington, Cossack, Dainty, Daring, Defender, Deitelnyi (ex-Churchill), Delight, Diamond, Duchess, Dulverton, Eclipse, Electra, Encounter, Escort, Esk, Eskdale, Exmoor, Exmouth, Fearless, Firedrake, Foresight, Fury, Gallant, Gipsy, Glowworm, Grafton, Grenade, Grenville, Greyhound, Grove, Gurkha (1), Gurkha (2) (ex-Larne), Hardy (1), Hardy (2), Harvester, Hasty, Havant, Havock, Hereward, Heythrop, Holcombe, Hostile, Hunter, Hurricane, Hurworth, Hyperion, Imogen, Imperial, Inglefield, Intrepid, Isis, Ivanhoe, Jackal, Jaguar, Janus, Jersey, Juno, Jupiter, Kandahar, Kashmir, Keith, Kelly, Khartoum, Kingston, Kipling, Kujawiak (ex-Oakley (1)), La Combattante (ex-Haldon), Laforey, Lance, Legion, Lightning, Limbourne, Lively, Mahratta, Maori, Martin, Mashona, Matabele, Mohawk, Nestor, Orkan (ex-Myrmidon), Pakenham, Panther, Partridge, Penylan, Puckeridge, Punjabi, Quail, Quentin, Quorn, Rockingham, Sikh, Somali, Southwold, Stanley, Stronghold, Sturdy, Svenner (ex-Shark), Swift, Tenedos, Thanet, Tynedale, Valentine, Vampire, Venetia, Veteran, Vimiera, Vortigern, Wakeful, Warwick, Waterhen,

Wessex, Whirlwind, Whitley, Wild Swan, Wren, Wrestler, Wryneck, Zulu.

Summary
Mined: 23
Aircraft attack: 50
Sunk by U-boat: 35 (see details below)
Surface action: 20
Shore batteries: 2
Collision: 3
Wrecked: 2
Blockship: 1
Accident: 1
Uncertain: 2
Total: 139

RN destroyers lost by enemy submarine attack, 1939-45

Attacked	By	Nationality
Bath	U201	German
Belmont	U82	German
Beverley	U188	German
Blean	U443	German
Broadwater	U101	German
Cossack	U563	German
Daring	U23	German
Churchill (later *Deiltelnyi*)	U956	German
Escort	Marconi	Italian
Exmouth	U22	German
Firedrake	U211	German
Grove	U77	German
Gurkha (2)	U133	German
Hardy (2)	U278	German
Harvester	U432	German
Heythrop	U652	German
Holcombe	U593	German
Hyperion	Serpente	Italian
Jaguar	U652	German
Laforey	U223	German
Mahratta	U956	German
Martin	U431	German
Matabele	U454	German

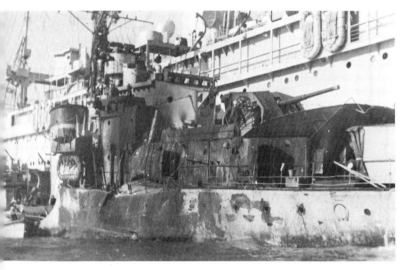

Views of HMS *Saumarez* (above left) and HMS *Volage* (left) after mining in 1946. Both struck mines in the international waters of the Corfu Channel. Both received great damage and HMS *Volage* had her bows blown off.
Both: J. Wilkinson

Attacked	By	Nationality
Myrmidon (later *Orkan*)	U610	German
Partridge	U565	German
Puckeridge	U617	German
Somali	U703	German
Stanley	U574	German
Tynedale	U593	German
Veteran	U404	German
Warwick	U413	German
Whirlwind	U34	German

Destroyer casualties caused by either Italian or German weapons similar to the Chariots and X-Craft of the Royal Navy are not included in this appendix.

Torpedo boat destroyers and destroyers lost in time of peace

Ariel 'D' class, at Ricasoli was wrecked on the breakwater whilst testing harbour defences on 19 April 1907.

Blackwater, 'E' class, sank after colliding with the ss *Hero* on 6 April 1909 off Dungeness.

Cleveland, 'Hunt' Type 1, whilst on passage off Swansea on 28 June 1957 was stranded and became a total loss, being finally blown up on 14 December 1959.

Cobra, 'C' class, went ashore near Cromer, on 19 September 1901.

Decoy, 'A' class, sank on 13 August 1904 after colliding with HMS *Arun* off the Wolf Rock.

Gala, 'E' class, sank after colliding with HMS *Attentive* off Harwich.

Lee, 'C' class, was wrecked on 5 October 1909 near Blacksod Bay.

Salmon, 'A' class, sank on 2 December 1901 after colliding with ss *Cambridge* at Harwich.

Sparrowhawk, 'B' class, was wrecked on 17 June 1904 at the mouth of the Yangste River.

Speedy, Thornycroft 'S' class, sank on 24 December 1922 after colliding with a tug in the Sea of Marmora.

Stonehenge, Admiralty 'S' class, was wrecked on 6 November 1920 off Smyrna.

Tiger, 'E' class, sank on 2 April 1908 after colliding with HMS *Berwick* off St Catherines.

Viper, 'C' class, went aground on Bushan Island off Alderney on 3 August 1901.

Walrus, Admiralty 'V' class, was wrecked on 12 February 1938 in Filey Bay, refloated 29 March and broken up in October 1938.

Summary
Collision: 6
Wrecked: 8
Total: 14

5 Submarines sunk by RN Destroyers

German submarines 1914-18

U-boat	Date of attack	Details
U-8	4 March 1915	HMS *Gurkha* and *Maori* in the Straits of Dover.
U-12	10 March 1915	HMS *Ariel*, by ramming, off Aberdeen.
U-48	24 November 1917	HMS *Gipsy* and five of HM trawlers by shellfire, *U-48* being stranded on the Goodwin Sands.
U-69	12 July 1917	HMS *Patriot* in the North Sea.
UB-29	6 December 1916	HMS *Ariel*, 12 miles south-west of the Bishop Rock Lighthouse.
UB-70	8 May 1918	HMS *Basilisk*, and the USS *Sydonia* (?) off Malta.
UB-110	19 July 1918	HMS *Garry*, north-west of Spurn Point being later raised and salvaged by the RN.

U-boat	Date of attack	Details
UC-16	23 October 1917	HMS *Melampus*, off Selsey Bill.
UC-19	4 December 1916	HMS *Llewllyn* in the Straits of Dover.
UC-26	9 May 1917	HMS *Milne*, by ramming in the Thames estuary.
UC-46	8 December 1917	HMS *Liberty*, by ramming in the Straits of Dover.
UC-50	4 February 1918	HMS *Zubian*, by ramming in the North Sea.
UC-75	31 May 1918	HMS *Fairy*, by ramming in the North Sea.

German submarines 1939-45

U-boat	Date of Attack	Details
U27	22 September 1939	HMS *Forester* and *Fortune* west of the Hebrides.

U-boat	Date of attack	Details
U31	2 November 1940	HMS *Anthony* in north Atlantic. (*U31* had been previously sunk on 11 March 1940 by Allied aircraft in the Schillig Roads. She was raised, refitted and recommissioned.)
U32	30 October 1940	HMS *Harvester* and *Highlander* in the North Atlantic.
U35	29 November 1939	HMS *Icarus*, *Kashmir* and *Kingston* north west of Bergen.
U39	14 September 1939	HMS *Faulknor*, *Firedrake* and *Foxhound* north-west coast of Ulster.
U41	5 February 1940	HMS *Antelope* off the southern coast of Eire.
U42	13 October 1939	HMS *Ilex* and *Imogen* off the south-west coast of Eire.
U44	20 March 1940	HMS *Fortune* off the north coast of Shetland.
U45	14 October 1939	HMS *Inglefield*, *Intrepid* and *Ivanhoe* off the coast of Eire.
U49	15 April 1940	HMS *Fearless* off Narvik.
U50	10 April 1940	HMS *Hero* off the north coast of Shetland.
U53	21 February 1940	HMS *Gurkha* (1) off the coast of Orkney.
U55	30 January 1940	HMS *Whitshed*, *Fowey* (sloop) and aircraft south-west of the Scillies.
U63	26 February 1940	HMS *Escort*, *Imogen* and *Inglefield* off the south coast of Shetland.
U69	17 February 1943	HMS *Viscount* in the North Atlantic.
U70	8 March 1941	HMS *Wolverine* off the south coast of Iceland.
U74	2 May 1942	HMS *Wishart*, *Wrestler* and aircraft off the coast of Cartagena.
U75	28 December 1941	HMS *Kipling* off the coast of Mersa Matruh.
U76	5 April 1941	HMS *Wolverine* with *Scarborough* (sloop) off the south coast of Iceland.
U79	23 December 1941	HMS *Hasty* and *Hotspur* off the coast of Tobruk.
U87	4 March 1943	HMCS *St Croix* and *Shediac* (frigate) south of Oporto.
U88	14 September 1942	HMS *Onslow* south of Spitzbergen.
U89	14 May 1943	HMS *Broadway* with *Biter* (Escort carrier) and *Lagan* (frigate) and aircraft from *Biter* in mid-Atlantic.
U90	24 July 1942	HMCS *St Croix* off Newfoundland.
U93	15 January 1942	HMS *Hesperus* north of Madeira.
U99	17 March 1941	HMS *Walker* south of Iceland.
U100	17 March 1941	HMS *Vanoc* and *Walker* south of Iceland.
U110	9 May 1941	*U110* was depth charged with such effect that she surfaced and surrendered and she was boarded, the crew transferred to HM ships and made safe for towing to a UK port but due to damage sustained during the attacks and possible sabotage by her crew she foundered in tow. HMS *Broadway*, *Bulldog* and *Aubretia* (corvette) were the attackers.
U131	17 December 1941	HMS *Blankney*, *Exmoor* and *Stanley* with aircraft from *Audacity* (escort carrier), *Stork* (sloop), and *Penstemon* (corvette) west of Madeira.
U138	16 June 1941	HMS *Faulknor*, *Fearless*, *Foresight*, *Forester* and *Foxhound* in the north Atlantic.
U147	2 June 1941	HMS *Wanderer* and *Periwinkle* (corvette) north west of Eire.
U162	3 September 1942	HMS *Pathfinder*, *Quentin* and *Vimy* off Trinidad.
U179	8 October 1942	HMS *Active* off Cape Town
U186	12 May 1943	HMS *Hesperus* north of the Azores.
U187	4 February 1943	HMS *Beverley* and *Vimy* in the north Atlantic.
U191	23 April 1943	HMS *Hesperus* in the north Atlantic.
U201	17 February 1943	HMS *Fame* off Newfoundland.
U203	25 April 1943	HMS *Pathfinder* and aircraft from *Biter* (escort

U-boat	Date of attack	Details	U-boat	Date of attack	Details
		carrier) south of Greenland.			(destroyer escorts) and FFS *Senegalais* (frigate) off the Algerian coast.
U205	17 February 1943	HMS *Paladin* and aircraft off Malta.	*U372*	4 August 1942	HMS *Croome, Sikh, Tetcott* and *Zulu* and aircraft off Jaffa.
U207	11 September 1941	HMS *Leamington* and *Veteran* south of Greenland.	*U381*	19 May 1943	HMS *Duncan* and *Snowflake* (corvette) south of Greenland.
U223	30 March 1944	HMS *Blencathra, Hambledon, Laforey* and *Tumult* north of Palermo.	*U390*	5 July 1944	HMS *Wanderer* and *Tavy* (frigate) in Seine Bay.
U229	22 September 1943	HMS *Keppel* south of Greenland.	*U392*	16 March 1944	HMS *Vanoc* and *Affleck* (frigate) and aircraft in the Straits of Gibraltar.
U242	30 April 1945	HMS *Havelock* and *Hesperus* in the Western Approaches.	*U394*	2 September 1944	HMS *Keppel, Whitehall* and *Affleck* (frigate) and aircraft from *Vindex* (escort carrier) west of Harstadt.
U274	23 October 1943	HMS *Duncan* and *Vidette* and aircraft south-west of Iceland.			
U282	29 October 1943	HMS *Duncan* and *Vidette* and *Sunflower* (corvette) in mid-Atlantic.	*U401*	3 August 1941	HMS *St Albans, Wanderer* and *Hydrangea* (corvette) south-west of Eire.
U289	31 May 1944	HMS *Milne* south-west of Bear Island.	*U407*	19 September 1944	HMS *Garland, Terpischore* and *Troubridge* south of Milos.
U305	17 January 1944	HMS *Wanderer* and *Glenarm* (frigate) south-west of Eire.	*U409*	12 July 1943	HMS *Inconstant* north of Algiers.
U306	31 October 1943	HMS *Whitehall* and *Geranium* (corvette) north of the Azores.	*U411*	15 November 1942	HMS *Wrestler* off Bone.
			U413	20 August 1944	HMS *Forester, Vidette* and *Wensleydale* south of Brighton.
U314	30 January 1944	HMS *Meteor* and *Whitehall* south of Bear Island.	*U434*	18 December 1941	HMS *Blankney* and *Stanley* north of Madeira.
U325	30 April 1945	HMS *Havelock* and *Hesperus*, south Irish Sea.	*U443*	23 February 1943	HMS *Bicester, Lamerton* and *Wheatland* off Algiers.
U340	1 November 1943	HMS *Active, Witherington* and *Fleetwood* (sloop) and aircraft in the north Atlantic.	*U444*	11 March 1943	HMS *Harvester* and FFS *Aconit* (corvette) in mid-Atlantic.
U344	24 August 1944	HMS *Keppel* and *Loch Dunvegan* (frigate) and *Mermaid* and *Peacock* (sloops) north of North Cape.	*U450*	10 March 1944	HMS *Blankney, Blencathra, Brecon* and *Exmoor* off Anzio.
U353	16 October 1942	HMS *Fame* in mid-Atlantic.	*U453*	21 May 1944	HMS *Liddesdale, Termagant* and *Tenacious* north of Sardinia.
U355	1 April 1944	HMS *Beagle* and aircraft from *Tracker* (escort carrier) south-west of Bear Island.	*U457*	16 September 1942	HMS *Impulsive* north of Murmansk.
			U458	22 August 1943	HMS *Easton* and RHN *Pindos* south of Pantellaria.
U357	26 December 1942	HMS *Hesperus* and *Vanessa* north-west of Eire.	*U472*	4 March 1944	HMS *Onslow* and aircraft from *Chaser* (escort carrier) south of Bear Island.
U360	2 April 1944	HMS *Keppel* north-west of Hammerfest.			
U371	4 May 1944	HMS *Blankney* and USS *Pride* and *Campbell*	*U523*	25 August 1943	HMS *Wanderer* and

U-boat	Date of attack	Details
		Wallflower (corvette) west of Vigo.
U531	6 June 1943	HMS *Oribi* and *Snowflake* (corvette) north of Newfoundland.
U559	30 October 1942	HMS *Hero*, *Hurworth*, *Dulverton*, *Pakenham* and *Petard* and aircraft north of Port Said.
U562	19 February 1943	HMS *Hursley* and *Isis* and aircraft north of Benghazi.
U568	28 May 1942	HMS *Eridge*, *Hero* and *Hurworth* north of Tobruk.
U581	2 February 1942	HMS *Westcott* south-west of the Azores.
U585	29 March 1942	HMS *Fury* off Vardo.
U587	27 March 1942	HMS *Aldenham*, *Grove*, *Leamington* and *Volunteer* in mid-Atlantic.
U589	12 September 1942	HMS *Faulknor* south-west of Spitzbergen.
U593	12 December 1943	HMS *Calpe* and USS *Wainwright* off Constantine.
U619	15 October 1942	HMS *Viscount* in mid-Atlantic.
U621	18 August 1944	HMCS *Chaudiere*, *Kootenay* and *Ottawa* off La Rochelle.
U651	30 June 1941	HMS *Malcolm* and *Scimitar* with *Violet*, *Speedwell* and *Arabis* (corvettes) south of Iceland.
U671	4 August 1944	HMS *Wensleydale* and *Stayner* (destroyer escort) south of Brighton.
U678	6 July 1944	HMCS *Kootenay*, *Ottawa* and HMS *Statice* (corvette) south of Brighton.
U713	24 February 1944	HMS *Keppel* north-west of Narvik.
U719	26 June 1944	HMS *Bulldog* in the north Atlantic.
U732	30 October 1943	HMS *Douglas* and *Imperialist* (trawler) off Tangiers.
U744	6 March 1944	HMS *Icarus* and HMCS *Chaudiere* and *Gatineau*, with *Kenilworth Castle* and HMCS *St Catherines* (frigates) also *Chilliwack* and *Fennel* (corvettes) in mid-Atlantic.
U761	24 February 1944	HMS *Anthony* and *Wishart* with aircraft off Tangiers.
U767	18 June 1944	HMS *Fame*, *Havelock* and *Inconstant* south-west of Guernsey.
U845	11 March 1944	HMS *Forester* and HMCS *St Laurent* with HMCS *Owen Sound* and *Swansea* (frigates) in mid-Atlantic.
U878	10 April 1945	HMS *Vanquisher* and *Tintagel Castle* (frigate) west of St Nazaire.
U971	24 June 1944	HMS *Eskimo* and HMCS *Haida* and aircraft off Ushant.
U984	20 August 1944	HMCS *Chaudiere*, *Kootenay* and *Ottawa* west of Brest.
U1195	6 April 1945	HMS *Watchman* south of Spithead.
U1199	21 January 1945	HMS *Icarus* and FFS *Migonette* (corvette) off the Scillies.
U1274	16 April 1945	HMS *Viceroy* north of Newcastle.

Italian submarines 1940-43

U-boat	Date of Attack	Details
Adua	30 September 1941	HMS *Gurkha* (2) and *Legion* in the western Mediterranean.
Alissandro Malaspina	21 September 1941	HMS *Vimy* in the north Atlantic.
Amiraglio Caracciolo	11 December 1941	HMS *Farndale* off Bardia.
Ascianghi	23 July 1943	HMS *Eclipse* and *Laforey* south of Sicily.
Anfitrite	6 March 1941	HMS *Greyhound* off Crete.
Asteria	17 February 1943	HMS *Easton* and *Wheatland* of Bougie.
Berillo	2 October 1940	HMS *Hasty* and *Havock* off Alexandria.
Cobalto	12 August 1942	HMS *Ithuriel* and *Pathfinder* off Bizerta.
Dagabur	12 August 1942	HMS *Wolverine* off Algiers.
Dessie	28 November 1942	HMS *Quentin* and *Quiberon* (RCN) north of Bone.
Durbo	18 October 1940	HMS *Firedrake*, *Wrestler* and aircraft east of Gibraltar.

U-boat	Date of attack	Details	U-boat	Date of attack	Details
Evangelista Torriceli	22 June 1940	HMS Kandahar, Kingston and Shoreham (sloop) in the Red Sea.	Naide	14 December 1940	HMS Hereward and Hyperion off Bardia.
Faa di Bruno	8 November 1940	HMS Havelock in the north Atlantic.	Narvalo	14 January 1943	HMS Hursley, Pakenham and aircraft south-east of Malta.
Galileao Ferranris	25 October 1941	HMS Lamerton and aircraft in the north Atlantic.	Neghelli	19 January 1941	HMS Greyhound in the eastern Mediterranean.
Glauco	27 May 1941	HMS Wishart west of Gibraltar.	Nereide	13 July 1943	HMS Echo and Ilex in the Messina Straits.
Gondar	20 September 1940	HMS Stuart and aircraft off Alexandria.	Uebi Scebili	29 June 1940	HMS Dainty and Ilex off Crete.
Lafole	20 October 1940	HMS Hotspur, Gallant and Griffin east of Gibraltar.	Varsciek	15 December 1942	HMS Petard and Queen Olga (Greek) south of Malta.
Leonardo de Vinci	23 May 1943	HMS Active and Ness (frigate) north-east of the Azores.			
Liuzzi	27 June 1940	HMS Dainty and Ilex off Crete.			
Maggiori Baracca	8 September 1941	HMS Croome, north-east of the Azores.			

Japanese Submarines 1942-45

U-boat	Date of attack	Details
I60	17 January 1942	HMS Jupiter, 25 miles off Krakatoa.
I27	12 February 1944	HMS Paladin and Petard, 60 miles from Adu Attoll.

Bibliography

A. J. Watts; *Japanese Warships of World War 2*; Ian Allan Ltd, 1968.

J. C. Taylor; *German Warships of World War 2*; Ian Allan Ltd, 1966.

H. M. Le Fleming; *Warships of World War 1, No 3 Destroyers*; Ian Allan Ltd.

F. T. Jane; *Jane's Fighting Ships*; Various Editions, Sampson Low & Marston.

Peter Elliott; *Allied Escort Ships of World War II*; Macdonald & Janes, 1977.

Labayle Couhat; *Combat Fleets of the World 1976/77*; Arms & Armour Press.

R. V. B. Blackman; *The Worlds Warships 1955*; Macdonald.

H. T. Lenton; *British Fleet & Escort Destroyers 1 1970*; Macdonald.

Navy Losses 1919; HMSO

Mike Critchley: *British Warships and Auxiliaries 1979*; Maritime Books.

Alan Raven and John Roberts; *Ensign 6. War Built O to Z Class Destroyers*; Bivouac Books Ltd, 1975.

Capt T. D. Manning and Cdr C. F. Walker; *British Warship Names 1959*; Putnam.

Index of Ships' Names

Above: HMS *Glamorgan* on builders trials, testing her rate of advance. *MoD(N)*

Left: HMS *Norfolk* on builders trials and showing that she is fitted with two bow anchors, unlike the later Type 42s which have to manage with one. *MoD(N)*

Index of classes

Below: HMS *Devonshire*, 'County' class.   *MoD (Navy)*